Remember the Prisoners

Remember
the
Prisoners

edited by
Peter Masters

MOODY PRESS
CHICAGO

© 1986 by
THE MOODY BIBLE INSTITUTE
OF CHICAGO

All Scripture quotations, unless noted otherwise, are from the King James Version.

Library of Congress Cataloging in Publication Data

#13795229

Remember the prisoners.

    1. Baptists—Soviet Union—Biography. 2. Prisoners—
Soviet Union—Biography. 3. Persecution—Soviet Union—
History—20th century. 4. Soviet Union—Church history—
1917-   I. Masters, Peter.
BX6493.R46   1986   286'.0947   86-12841
ISBN 0-8024-7388-1 (pbk.)

1 2 3 4 5 6 Printing/ LC /Year 91 90 89 88 87 86

Printed in the United States of America

Contents

Preface

Twenty-five years ago a movement of churches began in the Soviet Union, which, despite intensive activity on the part of the authorities to eliminate it, has rapidly grown to more than two thousand congregations. Responsible for that growth is a nationwide fellowship of Baptist congregations that refuse official registration and recognition because of the repressive conditions that are attached. Throughout this book we call them "unregistered Baptist churches."* The movement began when a number of churches seceded from the officially recognized Baptist denomination because they refused to suffocate under the blanket of government restrictions designed to extinguish all effective Christian witness.

Their road has not been easy. Church members have endured thousands of prison sentences, fines, interruptions of services, and house searches. Parents have been deprived of the custody of their children, and a number of young men have been so brutally beaten that they have died from their injuries. Some believers have been shut away indefinitely in psychiatric institutions for the criminally insane.

---

*Their proper denominational title is "The Council of Evangelical Christian Baptist Churches." This title was derived from the fact that the congregations elect a council composed of leading pastors to organize certain shared activities such as the clandestine publishing work. This large group of churches must not be confused with the "All-Union Council of Evangelical Christian Baptist Churches," which is the name of the *officially recognized* Baptist denomination strictly monitored by the authorities.

In these pages a number of leading pastors and key workers tell the stories of their struggles to proclaim their message no matter the cost. They tell of their own spiritual experiences, of lives transformed by the blessing of God, and of their trials and sorrows. Some are young men and women who have given their years of youth to health-ravaging concentration camps. We read of the rigors of interrogation prisons and punishment cells and of the tensions of working for the underground printing presses, which supply huge quantities of Bibles to Russian believers. Surely here are the present-day heroes of faith, of whom the world is not worthy.

The purpose of this book is to move the hearts of Christians living in freedom so that they may pray for these persecuted believers and be challenged by their dedication and sacrifice. This book is in no way intended to arouse political passions or to fuel the fires of political debate, for these persecuted believers do not assume a political or anti-government stance. They are not dissidents in the usual sense of the term, but simply believers who feel bound to obey God rather than man and to honor Christ's Great Commission to preach His gospel. As loyal citizens they ask for nothing more than the liberty that the constitution of the USSR is supposed to give them—the liberty to follow and proclaim their faith unhindered by restrictions and persecution.

From time to time stories of doubtful authenticity about persecuted Soviet believers appear in Western publications. One reads of extraordinary events and amazing miracles that, by their very style of narration, lack the ring of truth. Such tales slip into the pages of certain books and magazines as if from nowhere, and the people portrayed are never heard of again. The people whose testimonies you will read in this book are real people who live in the places mentioned and wear prison uniforms in the camps described. We feel we know them, for we have followed their affairs closely over a number of years. We have their letters, their photographs— even motion picture films and recordings of their voices. We

know their addresses and many of their relatives and compa-
triots-in-suffering who have migrated to the West and who
authenticate these events.

Most of our information has come from an organization
within the USSR called the Council of Prisoners' Relatives.
You will read about this remarkable group of women who document the prison sentences and other persecutions experienced by Russia's unregistered Baptist believers. Everything
you will read has originated from and has been attested to by
such trustworthy sources.

May this book move many hearts, inspire many prayers,
and call many believers to greater earnestness and commitment in the service of the King of kings.

Acknowledgments

The editor is indebted to the following sources for articles and information included in this work:

Byulleteni Soveta Rodstvennikov Usnikov E.Ch.B. (*Bulletin of the Council of Prisoners' Relatives of the Evangelical Christian Baptists,* USSR)

Vestnik Istiny (*Herald of Truth* magazine, issued by the clandestine press of the E.Ch.B. churches, USSR)

Nachrichten von den Feldern der Verfolgung (*News from the Fields of Persecution,* issued by the Missionswerk Friedensstimme, Gummersbach, West Germany)

1

The Church Soviet Authorities Designed

Gennadi Kryuchkov was one of the pastors who in 1961 led many Baptists out of the state organized denomination, despite great persecution, to experience renewal and revival. As president of the Council of Unregistered Baptist Churches he is forced to work underground. He has lived at home for only eighteen months in the last twenty-five years because of constant police surveillance. Pastor Kryuchkov is the only council member to have escaped discovery and imprisonment during the last five years. Yet because of the influence of his ministry in print he is unquestionably the KGB's most wanted Baptist. He was in prison from 1966 to 1969 and is now sixty years old. In the words that follow, Pastor Kryuchkov describes how the Soviet authorities created the official Baptist denomination in the USSR and how the Lord worked in the hearts of a large number of pastors, leading them to obey their Savior's commission regardless of the cost.

PASTOR KRYUCHKOV'S STORY

From the Scriptures we know that when the Lord's people are ruled by the Holy Spirit the churches grow and the preaching is blessed with success. Twenty-five years ago, however, our fellowship of Baptist churches was slowly dying, and congregations consisted of gray heads and wrinkled faces. We could have been called a "sisterhood" rather than a brotherhood, as four out of every five members were women in advancing years. The true cause of this situation did not lie in the difficult circumstances of our Russian environment. We now realize that it was because of our guilt: we were paying the heavy penalty for not having fulfilled the Great Commission of Christ. Our elderly congregations were the evidence of our betrayal of the Lord—the tragic fruit of our own apostasy.

An enemy had infiltrated our congregations like a cunning snake. He had assumed the form of a messenger of Christ and hypnotized us with the suggestion that the time was not right for a widespread proclamation of the gospel. It was constantly drummed into us that the appropriate course for us to pursue was the exploration and teaching of the depths of doctrine and experience rather than evangelization, but those depths proved so insubstantial that we became incapable of bringing even our own offspring to the Lord. Instead, we sacrificed them to the Moloch of our age.

We became afraid of the roaring lion and of men, and love grew cold within us because of our increasing disobedience. Then cowardice moved in, stealing our spiritual peace and bringing inner remorse. Lacking the Holy Spirit of freedom and truth, we began to suffocate spiritually until, subconsciously at first but gradually more consciously, God stirred our hearts, and we began to feel a new thirst for life and once again desire freedom in Christ.

We began the painful process of self-examination, realizing that while we were *near* the truth, we were not actually walking in it. We worshiped at our meetings, but we did not honor the Lord anywhere else—in our witness or in our lives. We came to see that our acts of worship were not done solely in obedience to the Lord, according to His commands, but that we heeded the enemy who forbade and limited our witness. Jesus Christ, the cornerstone of our spiritual building, had been driven out of the churches by the compromise of our church leaders.

We lacked the courage to make radical alterations, and even though we could see that the main structure was collapsing, we tried to repair our tottering building with minor modifications. Only when we repented of our sinful condition did we find freedom of spirit, genuineness in our relationships with each other, and peace and joy in the Lord.

The two Baptist denominations that existed before the revolution were the Baptists and the Evangelical Christians. These went on functioning for the glory of the Lord after 1917, and while they retained a measure of freedom for their activities, they had to obtain permission from and tolerate the interference of the state authorities on a number of issues. Then, in 1929, measures were taken by the authorities to intensify the fight against religion. Regulations were issued to control religious worship, and the activities of the two evangelical groups became severely restricted. Bible study courses were closed, publication of Christian periodicals and other Christian literature ceased, and large numbers of active believers were arrested. By the mid-1930s there were barely ten out of five thousand churches still in existence, and till the beginning of the World War II most believers were denied all opportunity to gather for worship and lived under constant repression. In other words, by the mid-1930s both of these groups of churches had effectively ceased to exist.

The question arises, How did the present officially recognized Baptist denomination, which is called the All-Union Council of Evangelical Christian Baptist Churches, come into being? And an equally important question is, Who laid down the constitution and basis of operation of the All-Union Council? It is certain that this organization did not result from the prayers and discussions of the Baptist or Evangelical Christian believers; it was created by the Soviet authorities. How and why did this new denomination come about?

The hardships of the war produced people who were seeking after God in many parts of the country, and, as a result, new life broke through in many areas at about the same time, like shoots through hard ground. Fellowships of committed Christians—some small, some large—sprang into being, and because of the severe opposition, ties between believers of this new generation were unusually close and firm.

Inevitably, the suspicions of the authorities were aroused, and measures were promptly taken to prevent these congregations from banding together under the leadership of preachers who were not servile towards the state. Then the Soviet authorities decided to form their own governing body to take control of the congregations. The new governing body was cunningly conceived. It would consist of respected officeholders representing the new congregations, yet they would be men who were ready and willing to collaborate with the authorities. But how were such people to be found? Most leading brethren were in concentration camps and prisons, and many had already died. Nevertheless, the authorities turned to the concentration camps. They searched for previously faithful servants of God who were enduring severe cold, hunger, and other sufferings in the camps. Any who were prepared to guide congregations under the direction of the authorities were offered their freedom.

Many of these brethren gave their word in writing that they would cooperate with the founding of a new denomination to take the place of the old Baptist and Evangelical Christian constituencies, both of which had been illegal for years. Consequently, in 1944 the new denomination of Evangelical Christian Baptists was formed, its officeholders being preachers whose spiritual loyalty had suffered shipwreck on the rocks of torture and imprisonment. Tragically, these brethren played their part in the great deception. The controlling body was called the All-Union Council of Evangelical Christian Baptist Churches, the first denominational hierarchy to be created by atheistic rulers.

Whatever genuine hopes the leading brethren may have entertained for this new denomination, they were not allowed to take a single independent step in their new roles. Once the German army had been driven out of the Soviet Union, various leading members of the new All-Union Council were sent to take over positions of leadership among the congregations.

Within a short time in the Ukraine alone, 170 congregations joined the new denomination; but as things turned out, only a third of these churches were later permitted to be registered, the others being compulsorily disbanded.

If the independent Baptist and Evangelical Christian congregations had only seen what was happening, they would have prayed for their preservation and taken a firm stand, but being inexperienced in the subtle ways of the secular powers, they thanked God for their apparent state recognition and freedom. They did not realize that this was not a victory *for* their congregations but a victory *over* their congregations.

It was soon clear that the new All-Union Council denomination had no divine origin. In no sense did its birth reflect the working of the Lord. It originated as a scheme of the Soviet authorities to aid them in their fight against the churches, and it was put into effect by the instrumentality of wartime labor camps.

It is possible that some of the brethren recruited to the All-Union Council hoped to maintain a faithful witness alongside a measure of cooperation with the state. Perhaps from that position they hoped to steer a course back to the paths of truth, but events only proved the impossibility of any such hopes. We now know many facts and possess many documents that prove the extreme anti-evangelistic policy of the All-Union Council. On the basis of this evidence we assert that the creation of the All-Union Council was the beginning of the end for numerous churches.

The state control of churches through the leadership of the All-Union Council is effected behind closed doors. Many of us have been behind those doors. To explain this statement I must touch upon a question that cannot be avoided, however sensitive it may be, for without an explanation of this point one cannot understand the horrifying calamity that struck so many congregations.

In 1956, when I was thirty years old, I was a candidate for a Bible study course abroad. The general secretary of the All-Union Council at that time, A. V. Karev, asked me to write down my testimony and life history. I did so and handed it to him. Shortly afterwards I was summoned to the police station where I was brought before high-ranking officials of the KGB.

As on many previous occasions, I refused to cooperate with them. After a long interrogation they said to me, "We do not want to change your convictions. You are a man with a settled view of life. But we know that your religious leaders are giving you a theological training to trust you with higher office. That is why we want to tell you that you're making a fatal mistake in being suspicious of us. Without us you will never progress one step in your work in the church."

That disturbed me deeply, for it revealed that spiritual leaders evidently had to conform closely with KGB requirements. But I was even more shocked to discover that spiritual officeholders sought to mislead church members into following their own policy of collaboration. Once while I was a deacon in the congregation at Uzlovaya I had a personal interview with A. V. Karev at the office of the All-Union Council.

"Well, brother, how is your work? What difficulties do you have?" he asked me.

"Thank God all is well, except that I'm being constantly summoned to talk with KGB officials," I answered.

"Well, what are they asking you?"

"They are demanding information from me about the life and activities of my church. They ask where the meetings are to take place; who is involved in running the youth work; what subjects are dealt with in the sermons; what visiting preachers we receive from elsewhere; what contributions are made in the deacons' meetings; and whether church members ever have guests in their homes without the police being notified."

"Well, brother, how did you react to all this?" Karev asked.

"It is obvious," I answered, "that as a Christian I cannot respond to such questions, but the Lord gives me the strength to stay faithful to Him."

Karev was silent for a while and then said, "You know,

brother, I would like to say one thing to you. You are unnecessarily afraid of your legal commitments. In our work, every duty, whether of a pastor, preacher, deacon, or choir leader, is fraught with legal obligations. Your overscrupulous straightforwardness does not help you. If you do not give such information, others will, and you will be pushed aside."

Horror gripped my soul in the face of the tragedy into which the Evangelical Baptist constituency had plunged, for if believers worked with their enemy, they would do so without God and would thus place themselves against God. What the state had founded was not a church but an anti-church.

Until that conversation, I believed that only some of the All-Union Council members played a double role. I had considered Karev an extraordinary person. When he had presented himself as a fervent preacher I had been carried along by his preaching, but suddenly I realized that his sermons had been empty words. The real man revealed himself behind closed doors. It was some time, however, before the full implications of what I had heard really took hold of me.

A number of brethren from our churches considered the predicament our constituency was in. We longed to know how we could please God and find the right path. Years went by, and it is uncertain how long this painful seeking would have lasted had not the black clouds of restriction drawn nearer. Repressive measures became stronger and stronger, and regulations were issued that further limited our work and our ability to evangelize.

It was not so much the repression that stirred us to take action, for repression can only bring blessings to churches that are right before God, but we were alarmed because we were facing persecution without the armor of God and His guidance. We had betrayed the commission of God, and in that condition we faced worsening persecution. Surely only defeat awaited us.

Thus we gradually came to recognize that only through repentance and change would we receive God's help to improve our churches. It became clear to us that God would not deliver us from persecution, but that He would restore our witness regardless of persecution if only we would be faithful to Him. This desire for a new attitude had already crystallized in the churches by the beginning of 1958. It became a full-fledged movement when an action group was formed to convene a conference of all Evangelical Christians to be held in the church at Uzlovaya in April 1961.

That action group began in the belief that the Lord would open the eyes of believers in the All-Union Council congregations to see the need for a complete change of direction. However, when we began our efforts to persuade our constituency to change course, we did not foresee the new directions and regulations about to be issued to the churches by the All-Union Council.

As soon as those were released, the eyes of many were opened to the sin of the All-Union Council, and their disastrous compromises became apparent. Among other restrictions the new directions ordered churches not to allow children to attend meetings, to severely restrict the number of baptisms of Christians under thirty years of age, and to end all cooperation with like-minded churches for joint meetings or visiting preachers. These directives stirred many true believers throughout the USSR to gasp at the enormity of their leaders' apostasy and to pray and fast for revival. In such circumstances the call of the action group was accepted by many Christians as a call from God.

Those of us who formed the action group naively cherished the hope that a tide of renewal would lead the All-Union Council members to repentance and the restoration of biblical practice. We therefore openly visited the office of the All-Union Council one month before the delivery of our initial publicity to the churches and had a long interview with A. V. Karev.

During the course of our interview, we said, "Your name is known the whole world over, for you are a man with great influence. We want to remind you as Mordecai did Esther—Did you not obtain such office so that you could raise your voice in defense of the truth of God and His people at a vital time?"

"You must understand that I cannot do that," he replied. "Besides, there is no point in it. Our organization has many levels of officeholders, and every position has a deputy position, and so on, many times over. If I stand out against the current situation, the other officers of the All-Union Council will inevitably gather for deliberation. Someone or another, be it Andreyev or someone else, will then discipline me for disorderliness. He will be supported, and I will be deposed. Someone else will continue the work in my place, and he may do it exactly the same way or even worse."

"In that case," we replied, "how in your opinion can the situation of our churches be improved?"

"We can no longer do anything. We gave the atheists the opportunity to put the noose around our necks, and now it is being drawn tighter every day," Karev answered.

This answer proved to us that our thinking was right, for Christ is the head of His church, and He allows no one to destroy her when she is faithful to Him. Persecution must never be identified as the cause of departure from the truth. The cause does not lie in the persecution but in our unfaithfulness. For that reason any improvement in the capacity of the churches to survive persecution must begin with repentance and change within the churches. The Scripture says, "Do not ye judge them that are within? But them that are without God judgeth" (1 Corinthians 5:12-13).

In 1962 our action group published the following reasons for wishing to organize a conference to stimulate change.

> We need this congress not for grand speeches but for a gathering of representatives from those local churches that look only to the teaching of the Bible and that will kneel before God and say, "Forgive us gracious God! Thou seest

how everything is so bad in our service, for many brethren have departed from Thy commandments, and we have looked on in indifference for so long that all Thy people are now suffering because of it. But now we have come before Thee, and ask for help to take the right direction according to Thy Word and Thy Holy Spirit. Send Thy Holy Spirit to revive Thy people that we might be pure and reunited according to Thy Word, and that we might be fit for Thy return."

The All-Union Council opposed the conference. Then, when the conveners of our conference were arrested, the All-Union Council took the opportunity to arrange their own conferences with a totally different emphasis. That was between the years of 1963 and 1966. Naturally, they did this with the fullest cooperation of the authorities.

The character of those All-Union Council conferences may be illustrated by the following incident. A brother who spoke at the All-Union Council conference in 1966 provided this testimony of his experience.

In the year 1966 I was chosen to take part in the congress of the All-Union Council, at which time I was also appointed to speak. I spoke about the great failure of the All-Union Council, about its departure from the truth, and about the kind of matters that the council leaders occupied themselves with.

After I had left the pulpit a man wearing a delegate's badge approached me and took me aside into a room. There he showed me his KGB pass. I asked, "Why are you here?"

He replied, "I am a member of the All-Union Council." Then he asked, "Who gave you the right to speak as you did? Who were you addressing yourself to? What are you scheming? Do you perhaps want to go back where you came from?" (By this last question the KGB officer was referring to an earlier prison term that I had served.) Then he added in a more cordial manner, "We want to be friends— here's my address."

I did not take the address but said to him, "I will speak to Karev about this." I went to Karev and told him everything. He embraced me and said, "It doesn't matter. You will get used to this with time. Things cannot work without them."

But when a similar congress was convened for 1969, I received a prior letter stating—"Do not attend the congress, so that there will be no unpleasantness. . . . "

Karev's words to the effect that every ministry is fraught with legal obligations are certainly true in the case of the activities of the All-Union Council. The atheists have caught many souls in this terrible net of compromise, as numerous testimonies show. I quote from a copy of a letter written to Karev by a brother who was in the ranks of the All-Union Council at the time. He handed this copy over to members of the action group council in 1966. The letter included these words:

> I am of the opinion that the principle root of sin that has put our churches in their present situation lies in the fact that All-Union Council members violate the divine principle of the separation of church and state. This principle clearly demands that people who are in the service of the church should not enter into secret relationships, compromises, or obligations with the state.
>
> The advice that you gave to me in the year 1958, when I came to you to collect Bibles for the church in Kiev and had a private conversation with you, shows that you are guilty of this very error. The Lord has cleared the way to our release and purification from such sins, and He has done this through the heroic deeds and sacrifice of many children of God. But why do you and all the others on the All-Union Council wish to persist in the error, and also to drag others down with you?

How can All-Union Council officers tell church conferences around the world that there is no persecution for the faith in our country? They know full well the terrible reality of the fight against religion that atheism is conducting through the courts of our country. The fight against religion that has been mounted ever since the revolution is, in scope and intensity, the worst in the history of mankind. It has been the cause of the sufferings of children as well as parents.

In the face of such reality the All-Union Council asserts the opposite statement: "After the announcement of freedom of conscience by the Soviet government, Evangelical Christian Baptists were able to continue their activities without hindrance. These activities included the proclamation of the gospel, the founding and strengthening of churches, the distribution of spiritual literature, and the training of church officers."

The reason for highlighting this lie of the All-Union Council is that this body still vehemently presses upon congregations the very code of practice that forbids such holy activities, and our people must be told why we cannot have any dealings with them or any fellowship with their members. The Soviet authorities recognized immediately that our challenge to the All-Union Council endangered their control over the churches, and so they employed every means at their disposal to restore the situation that suited them. Hundreds of our churches—those that followed the "no compromise" initiative—were oppressed by the authorities. Countless believers were tormented behind barbed wire.

One could easily feel that the powers that are mobilized against our movement are ludicrously excessive. Surely we are not worth such attention from the state! But in thinking along these lines we underestimate the great significance of our fellowship of churches. We are one of the few groups of churches of born-again Christians who insist on independence from the state. Our churches struggle only for fair independence, and though we do so with resolution, we have no hostility toward our persecutors. We strive because a life of conformity to this world is a sinful life.

We ask the world for nothing. We do not ask for any of its treasures. We are ready to lose all things, asking only one right for ourselves—the right to function as churches separated from the world according to the teaching of the Lord Jesus Christ—the right to be free from forced collaboration with the state.

2
From the Moment of Arrest

Passengers were told to stay in their seats after the Kirovabad flight landed at Rostov. Two men boarded the aircraft and moved through the cabin, scrutinizing every passenger. Soon they returned from the rear of the cabin escorting unregistered Baptist preacher Peter Peters, who was silent and pale. The authorities had wanted to catch this particular preacher for some time. As a traveling organizer and teacher of Baptist young people's groups, he had been greatly used of God and highly regarded and loved by congregations throughout the Soviet Union.

Among the passengers were several believers who had been unaware that Peter Peters was on board. When they disembarked, they attempted to speak to him as he sat in a police car on the runway, but they were pushed away by plainclothes officers. The prisoner was taken to a pretrial prison in Rostov to face for the fifth time months of interrogation, which he describes in the following pages. At forty-two years of age and having already endured four previous prison sentences, he was charged with spreading deliberately false inventions to slander the Soviet state.

The trial took place at Rostov in May 1984 and lasted just a few hours. Trials of believers often last several days, but in this case the authorities had no hope of obtaining any information from Peter or of making any impression on him, so they chose a quick trial to attract minimal attention. Few believers were allowed into the courtroom. Peter's brother Heinrich was one of the handful who got in.

Peter was still pale but seemed composed and even cheerful. After the main trial, the sentence was pronounced in a larger room into which more people were allowed. The custom on such occasions is for all those present to stand up when the presiding judge enters. Believers, however, have developed the custom of standing at an earlier moment— when their accused brother is brought in—both to show their respect and also to show him how many believers have come to support him in prayer. As Peter Peters entered the room, all the believers—a considerable proportion of those present —duly stood. The court officials were so surprised that one of them shouted, "All rise! The court is in session!" Unbelievers in the room also stood, only to find themselves greeting the prisoner with their respect.

The sentence was pronounced: three years in strict regime concentration camps. The judge had scarcely said the last word when Peter was showered with flowers. This was a powerful testimony to the boldness of the believers, for those who bring flowers into a courtroom risk fifteen days imprisonment and inclusion in the KGB's surveillance file. While the flowers cannot accompany the prisoner to his cell, the memory of such an act of affection, sympathy, and solidarity remains for a long time.

The following haunting description of what takes place after a believer's arrest was written by Peter Peters shortly before his most recent arrest and trial.

Peter's Story

Evangelical churches in the USSR are invited to take a broad road along which they will not be persecuted. Individual Christians are strongly tempted to take that road also, drawn by the sweet external freedom that it guarantees. Yet many believers will not take the road that avoids persecution and prison. Pastor Yakov Skornyakov, serving a fourth term of imprisonment, explains why.

> The Secret Service, which watches over believers, strives long and patiently to bring every pastor to one of two calamities. Either he must abandon his stand and work in his church in cooperation with the authorities, or he must permit his life, which is a thorn in their side, to be shortened. Believers, especially the active ministers and workers in churches, are treated as the enemies of the state, although as far as they are concerned, the state is not *their* enemy, for their only enemies are the devil and sin.

At the present time, prison doors separate hundreds of believers from those who are dearest to them because they will not yield to the flattering persuasion of state overseers. They will not behave more "reasonably" and comply with the requirements, which are designed to destroy churches. When a pastor or church worker is arrested and held for investigation, his mind is not so much occupied with the length or type of sentence he will receive as with the future of his local church. Questions crowd into his mind: *Will the fellowship stand fast under the pressures of persecution? Will the work of the kingdom come to a standstill because of the continuous night-and-day spying?*

He finds his heart filled with a desire for the well-being of the fellowship. He kneels in the smoke-filled, noisy cell and prays. Thinking of his fellow believers, he often goes without food to indicate to God the urgency of his prayers. Because of the unrestrained behavior of criminal prisoners it is almost impossible for him to concentrate on prayer. Anything spiritual is mercilessly ridiculed, dirty jokes are told, and swearing is constant.

Nevertheless, the arrested believer, whether young or old, a man or woman, must endure this for months before his trial while he is under investigation. During the day, scarcely any natural light penetrates the barred window covered by outside shutters. An electric bulb burns night and day so that guards can inspect the cell through the peephole.

After the daily walk in the prison yard, lasting for about thirty minutes, the believer becomes terrified to return to his cell, with its stench of stale nicotine. Immediately on return, those addicted to smoking will fill the small space with smoke. They smoke incessantly in that unventilated space as though they would rather suffocate than stop smoking. He can scarcely breathe, and his temples throb. Dr. Ivan Antonov recalled that, for him, "the craving for sleep was sheer torture. The only way to get to sleep was to place a wetted handkerchief, folded to several thicknesses, as a filter over the mouth and nose."

A prisoner may spend ten months or longer in these conditions while investigations continue. Throughout this time, he has no warm clothes in the winter and wears garments drenched and hardened by perspiration in the summer. He is often unable to bathe for months on end, receives no news from outside, and is unable to speak to anyone about his problems or feelings.

The prisoner is constantly pressured to accept the overtures of the authorities. He is offered the wonderful relief of freedom, without having to renounce the Lord, if only he will show a little more "insight." All he needs to do is to make one single concession, and that is to promise that he will join a registered church belonging to the All-Union Council of Evangelical Christian Baptists Churches. Then he may bid goodbye to his prison bunk forever. Pastor Sigarev was once offered his freedom on the condition that he would accept the pastorate of the registered church in Omsk.

Sometimes the secret overseers use a different approach to bring believers to give up their stand. Many Baptist prisoners at the present time are being offered their freedom without having to agree to go to a registered church. Instead, they are being asked to persuade their unregistered fellowship to register and accept the laws governing religious services. The overseers know that such a step will lead to a congregation's eventual spiritual collapse.

Lately, efforts to persuade imprisoned believers to follow this policy have been greatly increased. If the prisoner shows no sign of agreeing, he may be moved to another cell where violent prisoners have been urged to attack him. Thus pastors and other believers are cruelly beaten at the prompting of the secret overseers. After such an experience, the prisoner realizes he cannot be allowed visitors in his condition and is assailed by terrible despair at the thought.

The overseers will continue to plague him by a process of disorientation. The date of the trial usually is changed several times and kept secret from relatives. When, by some remarkable circumstance, friends do find out the date and come to the court, only a few of his closest relatives are allowed in. The others will wait outside to catch a brief glimpse of their dear brother in the faith as he gets out of the prison vehicle.

After the trial, the prisoner will usually face a prison posting designed to be brutally punishing in light of his circumstances and health. Pastor Volkov, who suffers from tuberculosis, was taken from Novorossiysk in the warm south and sent to Yakutien in the extreme north. Pastor Skornyakov and Yuri Seifert, who both suffer from ulcers, were each given black bread and a small portion of bad, salted herring for journeys lasting two or three days.

The rigors of transportation cannot be imagined. The prisoner who is transferred from the south to Siberia or the far east must often make the long journey in freezing conditions with only summer clothes because the secret overseers have forbidden him to be issued warm clothes and a coat. Even if a believer is arrested in winter and enters a cell with warm clothing, the organized harassment of inmates will leave him with only the few items of clothing that did not fit the gang leaders. The same can be said of food. Should the prisoner's relatives succeed in getting food through to him, he will not have much—if anything—after the usual compulsory sharing with the leaders in the cell.

After a prisoner has been moved from his hometown prison, his relatives will be told that he has been transported, say, to Yakutien. But that does not necessarily mean that he will arrive in Yakutien. He may be taken from the train at some point and sent elsewhere in order to keep his place of confinement a secret. This was done to Pastor Mikhail Khorev when he was sent to Omsk.

The prisoner may be detained in a transit prison and deliberately placed in a cell with particularly violent men who demand money from him. When he explains that he has none, they threaten to slash his arteries or hang him with a towel. Yet the Lord gives believers strength to endure such trials and helps them to commit their lives, their families and friends to His care and to face such threats with Christian calmn.

When the weakened prisoner arrives at his final destination, he falls into the rough hands of the camp administration. Here the authorities, following the directions of the secret overseers, make great efforts to reeducate Christians and to wean them from faith and prayer. A prisoner may be locked in a damp solitary confinement cell for months. The offense may be—as it was with Pastor Nikolai Boiko—a refusal to attend political classes. If a New Testament or a handwritten verse of Scripture is found during a search, that is enough to put the prisoner into solitary confinement.

Sergei Bublik was put into solitary confinement for writing down a Scripture text with notes.

"We have confiscated the notes," his interrogators said, "but is there anything more remaining in your head?"

"It is still there," the young man answered.

"You say it is still there?" the interrogators responded. "We will knock it out of your head."

Sergei was so severely beaten that both kidneys were damaged, and he became an invalid.

Living conditions in prisons are filthy. The prisoner soon

discovers that a single night on a tattered mass that only remotely resembles a mattress is enough to infest him with lice. The next day every stitch of his dirty clothing, and his body also, will be crawling with lice. Lice drop from his ears and forehead. Even after his clothing has been thoroughly baked—which only happens in a rare response to persistent pleading—the lice are not exterminated and soon reinfest and feed off his body. One pastor who has been imprisoned four times said that he has never been in a prison that was free from lice. Pastor Khorev, who once stayed a little longer than usual in the bath house to wash out his underwear that was stained by the squashed lice, was dealt such a blow that he could not sit down for a long time.

Alongside these rigors there is the agony of hunger. Scant rations do not replenish the effort expended on manual labor. The gnawing hunger forces the prisoner to think continually of eating, however hard he tries to put it out of his mind. He can hardly ever focus his mind to pray with the distress of his constant hunger. The cold, the moldy dampness, and the frozen concrete walls and floor of the solitary confinement cells all combine to rob the prisoner of the capacity to think clearly. To keep warm he must constantly keep moving and perform various physical exercises. It may be that the prisoner who is half-starved will be one of those to be struck off the list of those allowed to receive food parcels, as was the case with Sergei Bublik.

When the prisoner is awaiting a visit that has been approved, he is very closely observed during the days immediately preceding the date, and his belongings are searched. Should a New Testament or extracts from the Bible be found he will suddenly be told that the visit will be suspended. Relatives who have sometimes traveled thousands of miles with their children will be told this at the camp gates and will return with aching hearts and tears. Imagine what it must mean to a prisoner worn out by the oppressive atmosphere of blasphemy, but now lifted up in great anticipation of meeting with his loved ones, to have such hopes shattered at the very last moment. Alternatively, the long-awaited visit may be allowed, just so that it may be suspended after only a few minutes.

The Christian prisoner is usually classed with the worst criminal offenders by prison authorities and allocated the hardest and dirtiest work. The work quotas are fixed at a mercilessly high level, which not even a healthy, well-fed man could possibly fulfill. G. Arnautov had his glasses confiscated and then was ordered to weave nets. Mariya Tevs, an eczema sufferer, was forced to do laundry, which inflamed her condition and caused extreme pain. A pastor suffering from an ulcer was forced to melt pitch and was given a better diet only when his health was so bad that he could no longer eat at all. It is a simple fact that the believer is frequently treated far worse than criminal prisoners.

Pastor Pyotr Rumachik said to his wife when she visited him, "You are only allowed to stay with me for two days this time. They would have allowed us three days if it had been next month."

"Why did you not wait until next month?" Mrs. Rumachik asked wistfully.

To this Pyotr said with tears in his eyes, "Lyuba, Lyuba, I just do not know what will happen to me tomorrow."

In the midst of his difficulties, dangers, and painful trials, the prisoner must still bring the good news to those heading for destruction. He must try to tell the prisoners of Him who is more beautiful than all the sons of men, and who gave His life as ransom for many.

To see this side of a prisoner's life, read what one prisoner wrote about a harvest festival service that he convened in his cell for a group of men, one or two of whom had responded to his witness:

> In the evening we too held a harvest festival. We thanked God for that which we had before us—two onions, three pieces of salted fish, a handful of biscuits, a small cup of "sweets" made of white flour, three rations of black bread, and plenty of hot tea.
>
> It was to us a splendid feast for He joined in with us,

Who is love, and Who said, "Where two or three are gathered together in my name, there am I in the midst of them"
[Matthew 18:20]. It was a marvelous celebration of intimate
conversation in which prisoners laid bare the depths of their
fall into sin and sincerely sighed over their lost condition,
speaking also of the ray of hope that had shone into the
pitch darkness of their souls. It was not a service with solo-
ists and beautiful choirs. But it was a service in which those
present were awed and impressed by the content of what
was said and sung. When the hymn was sung, "Can You
Leave Without Having Turned to Christ?" a listening prisoner said, "Those words are just for me, write it down for me
if you can."

Then during the hymn, "In God's Assembly Is Perfect
Peace and Love, Why Then Delay, O Sinful Traveler?"—another prisoner said, "How I would like to be in such a gathering just to watch and listen." This was truly a festival of
sowing and reaping souls, and also a festival of sowing and
reaping the love of Christ.

In the face of his trials the prisoner can praise the Lord
for leading His people along the right road. With the eye of
faith, it seems to him that God has led him through beautiful
country in which he has found streams of God's blessing and
where Christ Himself surrounds him with a special love and
where His keeping hand accompanies him always. Never let
us forget in our prayers the names of such prisoners. May we
realize and remember that God alone can help His children to
go through the valley of the shadow of death without complaining.

No human patience, even in the most courageous and
resolute of people, would be sufficient to withstand all the ter-
rors of the persecutions and to maintain real joy and trust,
even to the extent of blessing the persecutors and not cursing
them. The apostle Paul teaches us that this cannot be done in
our own strength, but in Christ's strength alone, for in all
these things we are more than conquerors through Him that
loved us. In our Lord is the inexhaustible spring from which
our loved ones in prison draw strength and courage. To Him
be praise for everything.

*   *   *

An orchestrated program of persecutions has been un-leashed upon the Peters family for over three generations. Pe-ter's grandfather was seized by police in 1937—never to be seen again. His father, Daniel Peters, served a four-year sen-tence in a camp within the Arctic Circle in the 1940s. Peter's troubles began in 1947 when he was fifteen years old and had begun a course of study at a preliminary medical college in the southern Urals. Peter's Christian witness led him to expul-sion from the college within a single year, and he returned to his home village of Khortitsa where his earnest witness made a great impact on the young people.

The village authorities would not tolerate his activities and literally drove him out of the village. Peter was obliged to find a home somewhere else.

Then, in the 1960s, the Baptist churches were served with new rules and restrictions through their denominational leaders, who had compromised themselves with the Soviet Committee for Religious Affairs and accepted their demands.

In directives to the churches, the leaders ordered that children and young people should be excluded from the churches and that no church should have visiting speakers from other churches. Furthermore, only men approved by the authorities should preach.

The believers in the village where the Peters family lived refused to worship under those conditions and began to oper-ate as an unregistered church. Daniel Peters and his eldest daughter, Katharina, were consequently exiled to different vil-lages in Kazakhstan. The family followed their father into ex-ile. Later the family moved to a small settlement at Martuk, in the east.

At the age of twenty-two, Peter Peters was appointed to responsible service within the fellowship of unregistered churches. He could only rarely visit home. For months the family would know nothing of Peter's whereabouts. Then, one day in 1967, a letter arrived unexpectedly. It was a birthday letter from Peter to his little sister, but it came from a concentration camp. Only then did his family discover that he had been arrested and sentenced to two years' imprisonment. After his release he resumed his underground ministry among the churches.

In January 1973 the KGB tracked down a secret conference of unregistered Baptist leaders in Moscow. Peter was arrested and sentenced to three years' imprisonment for parasitism. According to Soviet law the ministers of any religious group may receive their income from the members, but in practice unregistered Baptist pastors and workers are frequently persecuted for parasitism if they are supported by the churches.

After two further years of freedom, during which Peter continued his ministry among the churches, he was again arrested and charged with parasitism. This time he was sentenced to spend two-and-one-half years in concentration camps. Before his release, Peter heard that his father, his brother Heinrich, and Heinrich's brother-in-law had all been arrested. On his release he went straight to his mother to support her, but she was convinced that he ought to return to his ministry among the churches and urged him to do so.

Peter attended the trial of his relatives with a heavy heart. Heinrich made a real impact upon the court. Humbly and simply he told of his path through life. He told the court that he had been known to all the inhabitants of Martuk as an alcoholic during the first five years after the family moved there. He spoke of how much evil he had done during that time and how the Lord had then stopped him in his tracks and made him a child of God. He related how, over the next five years, the community had seen the change in his life, and he added that he would certainly have come before the court for some serious crime if he had not found the Lord. Having spoken of his salvation, Heinrich was able to refute the charges made against him.

When the magistrates passed sentence, Peter's father received five years, Heinrich three years, and his brother-in-law three-and-one-half years. As the three prisoners were led out of the courtroom, the young Christians present threw flowers to them. A bouquet caught one of the guards, and this was later made the basis of fresh allegations against Peter Peters.

The first day after the trial, the wives of Heinrich and his brother-in-law went to the magistrates to obtain permission to speak to the prisoners. They also went to the public prosecutor's office to collect items that had been confiscated during the interrogations but were not subject to confiscation according to the court's sentence. The public prosecutor shouted at the wives and claimed that a piece of iron had been concealed in the bouquet that hit a courtroom guard. That was regarded as an attempt to kill the officer, and proceedings had been started to find and convict the culprit.

It became apparent that the public prosecutor was creating a case to bring against the new arrival in Martuk—Peter Peters. Alongside that, various other circumstances seemed to indicate that Peter's rearrest was imminent, and his relatives urged him to go underground immediately.

The day after he slipped out of Martuk he was being sought by KGB officers in Rostov-on-Don, where he had lived before his last imprisonment. Peter remained underground until the KGB found him in 1984. His father, Daniel Peters, was released in mid-1985.

The entire Peters family provides an example of the orchestrated troubles that are unleashed upon many key families in the Lord's work in the USSR. The difficulties and trials that they endure are not haphazard. Yet much fruitful soul-winning comes through the ministry and sacrifice of such families—fruit that grows out of suffering. "Except a corn of wheat fall into the ground and die, it abideth alone: but if it die, it bringeth forth much fruit" (John 12:24).

3
Galina's Ordeal

The ordeal of two twenty-one-year-old believers—Galina Vilchinskaya and Vladimir Rytikov—began early one morning as they returned from staffing a children's summer camp organized by the unregistered Baptists for the children of prisoners. Vladimir recorded the fateful moment.

At six o'clock in the morning of August 23, 1979, a group of about forty children accompanied by three adults were crossing the square in front of the railway station in Lvov. Every child carried a knapsack, for the group was returning home from a holiday trip. Suddenly uniformed men blocked their way, and one said, "Just a moment, citizens! A passenger has been murdered on the train that you've just left. You're under suspicion and must accompany us to the police station office."

As he spoke, some officers seized the adults while others collected their bags. The children, realizing the danger, slipped away from the scene quickly, and by the time the officers had finished arresting the adults, the children were nowhere to be seen. Four local people witnessed this incident in the station square, but they would not have realized that they had seen the arrest of three Baptist believers—my father Pastor Pavel Rytikov, Galina Vilchinskaya, and me. We had to wait several hours at the police station office; then a militia officer arrived who introduced himself as Major Statsendo, but later he told us that he was KGB Major Malyshev. Under guard we were taken to another police station where we were finally presented with a warrant for our arrest and taken to the cells.

For one month we were kept in these cells, constantly being interrogated by the investigating magistrate and KGB Major Malyshev. They wanted to know a great deal about the life of our church, and they wrote a great deal of purely fictitious material in the statements that they prepared for our signature. Naturally we refused to sign them. At first these interrogations were a great trial, but as time went by we were pressed to the point where we no longer reacted to their threats, demands, and screams.

After a month, Galina, Vladimir, and Pastor Rytikov were moved into the main prison at Lvov, where they remained until their trial. All were sentenced to three years normal regime imprisonment. Even before the trial a KGB major had threatened Galina, "I'll send you to where there are polar bears, and you will rot with no one knowing where you are."

Everyone in the Lvov prison knew Galina, for she passed through eight cells in her fourteen months there. Those who did not know her personally knew about her. Her poems and Christian songs had been copied down and passed from cell to cell. When word got around that Galina was being "sent to the bears," the inmates gave her whatever they had: a piece of sugar, a crust of bread, or a teaspoon of sugar wrapped up in paper. Of sugar alone she accumulated about six pounds by the teaspoonful.

In White Russia, where Galina's parents live (and in the Ukraine where she was sentenced), there are numerous camps for women. However, she was taken to the far eastern region, a place of extreme climate. On the exhausting two-month journey across the country from Lvov to Vladivostok, Galina went through nine transit prisons, experiencing cold, hunger, bed bugs, fleas, lice, and stench. She stayed in prisons where more than thirty prisoners were pushed into a cell designed for ten.

As usual there were thieves. When Galina left Lvov she had six bags, mostly the clothes sent by her parents during her fourteen months in prison. When she finally arrived at the concentration camp she had shared all her food, and everything else had been stolen.

She witnessed at every opportunity—in prison and in transit to the concentration camp. The camp authorities were annoyed and transferred her to another cell block, but she was not discouraged. She wrote home saying, "They want to punish me and hurt me. But I rejoice that even here I can witness about my Lord. I have listeners already, so I don't feel that I will last long here. But it doesn't matter, I am happy! By moving me around they are giving me the opportunity to evangelize my whole camp!"

At the investigation prison in Lvov, the KGB tried hard to get Galina to collaborate. Two months before her court hearing she was put in a cell on death row. The bunks were steel, and the walls, ceiling, and floor were bare concrete. The bread was terrible—doubtless made to produce painful effects. As Galina broke a slice in two, powdery sawdust-like matter flew out. After eating the bread she suffered sharp stomach pains. The Lvov prison is known for its cruelty. Prisoners sentenced to death are taken there for execution.

Galina was a little better off once she was sentenced and moved to a concentration camp. But her camp was located in low, rough hills in an uninhabited region thirty miles from the nearest village. The surrounding country harbored bears and even tigers, so none of the prisoners ever dreamed of escape.

With civilization so far away everything at the camp was very primitive. There was no plumbing, water was delivered in barrels, and washing and laundry were difficult and limited. Half the prisoners at this camp were convicted murderers, and all, with the exception of Galina, were natives to that part of the country. She alone had been sent 7,500 miles to this lonely spot. The climate was very difficult for her; the oxygen level was 16 percent below that which she was used to. When her mother visited her there, the temperature was -33°C (-27°F). To fly to the regional airport took eleven hours from Moscow.

One of Galina's letters home said, "I'm needed here more than in freedom. So many starving, suffering outcasts are here! Here in the far reaches of Russia there is more spiritual hunger than we have. I rejoice that in some small way I can help these Russian people who are drowning in sin."

Galina began life in the concentration camp in poor physical health, because during her year of detention before her trial she had received no hot meals—only a piece of bread each day with some raw fish. The malnutrition led to severe scurvy. Her hair fell out, her gums became inflamed, and she lost teeth. Her body became severely emaciated, and she developed chest pains and breathing difficulties.

In that state she began the rigorous program at the concentration camp. The prisoners were taken miles into the barren countryside and given manual labor to do for up to ten hours a day. Galina suffered cramps in her legs and was unable to sleep because of aching joints. Her boots did not dry out through that first winter. The barracks were not heated, and prisoners slept in their clothes.

Galina's mother tells of a visit to that far eastern concentration camp as Galina was into her second year of imprisonment.

> I traveled with my husband Vladimir to our second meeting with Galina in her concentration camp. He constantly expects arrest and wanted to see Galina once more before this might happen. The journey from the Ukraine to the far east was anything but pleasant. The thirty-mile stretch from Ussuriysk to the camp was especially difficult to cover. Only lorries traveled along the unbelievably bad road and we were forced to hitch lifts. Because there was never room for us in the cab, we were afraid that we would be thrown off the back of the lorry as it drove through the potholes. The cost of the journey alone came to one thousand rubles [a typical annual salary]. The authorities have sent Galina so far away from home deliberately in order to separate us completely. They counted on us not being able to visit her, but the Lord stands by us and gives us help through our friends.

We recently discovered that Galina's camp is the worst of all the women's camps with normal regime. There are 2,000 women there, 120 in Galina's barracks. Vladimir has also experienced imprisonment, but when he saw this camp he was horrified. The barracks in which the prisoners live resemble cow sheds that have become so dilapidated that they have been abandoned. They are full of holes and half-derelict. Living in them is simply unbearable, especially in winter [the time of this visit].

The prisoners are given a bowl of water each week, which is supposed to be sufficient for washing themselves, their clothing, and the bed clothes as well. This is, of course, impossible and within the prison community dirt leads to a continuous increase of fleas, lice, and bed bugs. When the women wake up in the mornings their faces and bodies are completely bitten. They have got so used to it that they hardly notice it. It is not possible to exterminate the vermin without sufficient water, and so no one even thinks about it.

The food is very bad also. In the morning they receive two spoonfuls of porridge made from oats or maize, a piece of bread, a glass of tea, and a spoonful of sugar. At midday they receive broth, with no solids in it, and a piece of bread to go with it. In the evening they again receive porridge, bread, and boiled water without sugar. So it goes on, day in, day out. On this diet the prisoners have to do ten hours hard labor every day.

Galina's health is somewhat better now. After her situation became known and people prayed, appeals reached the Soviet government and a doctor from the prison hospital in Vladivostok came to the camp and examined her. She was then immediately taken to hospital. Without these prayers and appeals we know she would never have got there. She was in the hospital for three weeks. However, some things are beyond cure, like the seven teeth she lost through scurvy. The swelling in her gums has almost disappeared and her stomach is also better now.

We cannot describe everything, but we rejoice that our daughter is still cheerful and continues to speak about the Lord to her fellow prisoners. When the opportunity arises she witnesses about her faith to her superiors also. To suppress her influence, the camp authorities move her round constantly from one section to another.

On the whole the women there have long sentences.

They are women who have fallen greatly and for whom there is no longer anything holy on earth. It is very difficult to live at peace with them. We had a conversation with the Camp Commandant Yakushevich and KGB Chief Malassay. The latter is especially hostile to Galina, even though she does not break the camp rules and achieves the work quota.

In reply to our asking why she does not receive our letters, he said very plainly: "If you mention God in your letters, she will not get them." Since our visit, already two months ago, Galina has not received a single letter. Not only the letters in which God is mentioned, but all others are being confiscated also, even unused paper and envelopes for replies. We have only received one letter from her, which was very short.

We ask our friends to pray for Galina, that she may live out the rest of her imprisonment with the same steadfastness and zeal for God. Galina asks us not to remain silent, but to do all we possibly can for her.

Galina was released from prison in August 1982, but within three months she was arrested again. While visiting young believers in Vladivostok she incautiously handed over her luggage at the luggage office at the station. Later she was subjected to a search, and drugs were found among her belongings. Prior to her being released from her previous prison term she had been threatened with arrest on charges that would have the effect of turning all believers away from her. KGB agents had kept their promise by planting the drugs in her luggage. At the beginning of 1983 Galina was sentenced to another two years in a concentration camp.

To understand the hostility of the authorities towards a girl in her early twenties one must look at the Vilchinsky family and the part they play in the unregistered Baptist church at Brest (Byelorussia). Mr. Vladimir Vilchinsky is a church deacon and a strong influence in the church against registration. The Brest congregation used to possess a building that the authorities tore down in 1960. Since then, nine church members have been imprisoned, and many members have been heavily fined for holding services in their homes. Believers have been persistently harassed at their work places, and some have been dismissed because of their church connections.

Almost five years ago a new campaign began to force this church to register. When Galina was first arrested in 1979, her father was mysteriously summoned by a local KGB officer, who proposed to him that his church should be registered. If Mr. Vilchinsky would persuade the church to register, the officer would arrange for Galina to be released from prison. This cooperation was refused, and Galina was duly sentenced to serve her prison sentence.

Upon her release from prison three years later another attempt was made to use Galina as a tool to secure the registration of the congregation at Brest. With two weeks of her sentence remaining, Galina was in a prison nearer home when she was called to the visiting block to see relatives. On arrival she found that there were no visitors, but she was bundled into a van and without being allowed to take any belongings was transported to her hometown of Brest. Before releasing her the authorities ordered her to join the registered church in Brest and also to bring her influence to bear on her father who was still "obstinately opposing" registration for the major portion of the Baptists in the town.

Galina went to stay with friends for a month to recuperate. Upon her return she was summoned to the public prosecutor's office, threatened with renewed arrest, and again told to join the registered church. As Galina was leaving the public prosecutor's office she was approached by a KGB officer who asked to speak with her. When she declined, he threatened to disgrace her among believers on account of her immoral behavior in the concentration camp. He shouted after her, "Watch out! It will be bad for you! You'll remember this when you get hurt!"

Soon afterwards Galina received invitations from believers in Ussuriysk and Vladivostok to visit them at their expense, and she set off on the long journey involving several flights. The authorities evidently monitored this journey carefully, for a believer in Vladivostok was questioned about Galina by a KGB officer before her arrival. The officer was carrying a photograph of her and described her as a "dangerous Baptist" who had previously served a prison term.

Galina was arrested in the night as she was about to begin her journey home. She had with her a collar of badger skin, some muskrat pelts (worth about ten rubles each), and a small mink fur, all these being presents from young people. She had nothing of value and no valuable sable skins.

Clear evidence that the KGB network had planned Galina's arrest may be gleaned from the way in which the news was used in Brest the very next morning. The district officer for religious affairs in Brest, Officer Sergeyev, summoned the elders of the *registered* Baptist church to tell them that Galina had been arrested for the illegal possession of drugs and valuable sable skins. The authorities clearly wanted to use the registered church to spread false charges that would bring the Vilchinsky family into disrepute and undermine the unregistered cause.

A month later the authorities searched the home of Galina's parents and also the home of her elder sister, saying that they were looking for drugs. Christian literature and cassettes were confiscated. The militia carrying out the search made the explicit statement that they were acting on KGB orders.

Galina's rearrest had undoubtedly been planned by the KGB because she, her parents, and over two hundred believers in their church would not agree to be registered and to conform to the regulations controlling worship and church activities. In the spring of 1984, Galina, in a concentration camp at Zaozernoye, was deprived of her right to receive long visits on the grounds that she had infringed concentration camp rules.

A few months later, in August, Galina spent her twenty-sixth birthday facing a session of intense KGB harassment, which all Christian prisoners have to reckon with in the months leading up to their release. Would she persuade her church to register? Would she cooperate with the authorities?

Galina Vilchinskaya was released from prison in the far-eastern Khabarovsk region of the USSR in November 1984. On the evening of her release she was able to take part, accompanied by her mother, in a gathering of believers in Khabarovsk. Local KGB officers were obviously anxious to see Galina moved out of their area as quickly as possible, for they even offered help in getting airplane tickets to expedite her journey home to Brest.

Galina and her mother flew to Moscow and then took the twelve-hour rail journey to Brest. Her father, in the meantime, had been interviewed several times by the police and warned against any kind of welcome home meeting for his daughter. However, the members of the unregistered church did gather to welcome and embrace Galina on her return, and on the next Sunday a very large number of young people visited Brest to greet her at the services. The morning service passed without interruption, but during the course of the afternoon service militia officers arrived and ordered the congregation to terminate their proceedings immediately. Naturally they did not comply. The following day Galina was fined fifty rubles for being the cause of the "disorder," an identical fine being imposed on both her father and mother.

Galina left prison in very poor health. Those around her said that she was so emaciated that she looked like an eleven-year-old child. Her facial skin was jaundiced in appearance, and her hair had become very thin. As in the case of others released from particularly harsh prison treatment, it was noticeable that every smile faded very quickly from her face, leaving her looking strained and gaunt. (However, immediately upon release she was made aware of the continuing stress she would be under. She was ordered to report regularly to police headquarters and forbidden to be out of her home between the hours of 8:00 P.M. and 6:00 A.M. for a period of at least a year.)

In October 1985, less than a year after her release from

prison, Galina was married to Ivan Shapoval at Brest. The authorities were present, and everyone was apprehensive, anticipating interference, but the event was allowed to go off peacefully. This is most unusual, especially when well-known believers are involved. Many wondered whether the receipt of a number of telegrams from overseas—doubtless monitored —may have indicated to the authorities that considerable interest was focused upon this young couple. Still they are marked out for intimidation for as long as they refuse to comply with the limitations placed upon believing churches.

How long will either Galina or Ivan be free? How soon will Galina, scarcely recovered and bearing in her body the effects of years of suffering, be taken back into the harsh confines of a concentration camp?

4

The "Crimes" of Unregistered Baptists

As recently as 1985, Alexei Bychkov, the present general secretary of the officially approved Baptist denomination in the USSR, wrote these words in a Russian magazine:

> We are fully satisfied with the relationship between church and state. Long ago, the path trod by our brothers and sisters was tragic and thorny. In czarist Russia, when the orthodox faith was the state religion, Baptists were persecuted. Many of them suffered imprisonment, exile, and other deprivations. Officials of the czarist regime closed their churches. Believers therefore welcomed the October Revolution and the Lenin decrees about the equality of all religions with great enthusiasm. Since then, Baptists have enjoyed equal rights as citizens of this country.

There can be no doubt that a man in Bychkov's position works in close cooperation with the KGB and that he is bound to say and write whatever is expected of him. His statement is typical of the campaign to discredit unregistered Baptists both to the general public in the USSR and overseas. They are depicted as an unreasonable, cultlike group of people who refuse to take advantage of the freedom of religion available to them, and it is repeatedly claimed that they suffer not because they are Christians but because they commit various criminal offenses.

The truth is that there is no freedom for believers who wish to worship and witness according to the teaching of the

Bible. If they will not accept the heavy restrictions upon all spiritual activities that are imposed upon registered churches, then they are charged with a formidable range of crimes and constantly hounded as criminals. Here are some of the crimes that have taken thousands of believers from unregistered churches to concentration camps over the years:

- Organizing any religious activity not under the auspices of an official recognized and registered church
- Taking part in services and prayer meetings of unregistered churches, as well as weddings, funerals, baptismal services, and young people's camps
- Speaking openly about personal faith or publicly preaching the gospel—often leading to a charge of "deliberately spreading falsehoods"
- Organizing Sunday schools
- Giving systematic religious teaching to children at home—even the writing of religious verse for one's children has resulted in a conviction
- Printing, storing, or distributing Christian literature
- Resisting a representative of the state or exhibiting willful disobedience to the authorities—believers commit this crime if they do not immediately respond to a command to stop praying or singing when a service is being broken up
- Making one's house available for Christian meetings
- Refusing to collaborate with the KGB when, for example, one is ordered to persuade one's church to seek registration or to give regular information about "overzealous" members, visiting preachers, church projects, and so on
- Working for the Council of Prisoners' Relatives; publishing and spreading information about Christian prisoners
- Parasitism or vagrancy, which is often charged to a newly-released prisoner who cannot get immediate work and is therefore given aid by other believers, or the preacher who receives any expenses or support from others
- Refusing to take the military oath, which is charged to many young believers when they go to their national service
- Rowdiness or disorderly behavior, which is charged when hymns are sung loudly at indoor meetings or at open-air assemblies in the woods

- Visiting, helping, or giving financial aid to other believers such as the sick and the elderly
- Attending the trials of fellow believers
- Engaging in an illegal craft, such as binding books (or more precisely, Bibles), other than under the auspices of a state-approved manufacturing process

To organize religious meetings other than under the auspices of a state-monitored, registered church is a serious crime, which in a single year brought sentences of up to six years to seven members of the unregistered Baptist church at Nikolayev. The indictment said that the church had evaded registration, ignored the laws governing religious practices, maintained links with similar churches, and operated an illegal fund for paying fines and buying banned Christian literature.

Clearly, with two thousand congregations, unregistered Baptists are not faced with long sentences like these every time they hold services. Most churches experience fairly regular arrests that result in fines or short, fifteen-day detentions. However, in any year a total of between fifty and eighty arrests will be made for this particular offense, which will lead to sentences of between two and six years.

Yevgeni Pushkov is a preacher at the unregistered Baptist church in Khartsyzsk. Yevgeni had just arrived home from completing a prison sentence when he was served with an official warning from the town executive that read:

> Citizen Pushkov: You are an active member of the religious society affiliated with the Council of Evangelical Baptist Churches, which acts contrary to the law. . . . You have been reported as an active participant in illegal religious gatherings on several occasions. . . . The executive committee of the town of Khartsyzsk hereby warns that if you and your colleagues . . . continue to hold your illegal gatherings, the records . . . will be forwarded to the public prosecutor's office. . . . We prescribe that you submit an application for the registration of your church activities within ten days.

None of the church members were prepared to apply for registration, for even if it had been granted they never would have accepted the clamping down on their witness. Neither would they have accepted the imposition of a pastor who collaborated with the local authorities. Within a fortnight Yevgeni was rearrested. He was sentenced to four years strict regime imprisonment, later revised to five years.

These cases are just examples of many pastors and other believers who have been imprisoned simply for organizing meetings outside the state-controlled denomination. To be a pastor among the unregistered Baptists could merit a sentence of three to five years. Vladimir Zinchenko is a young preacher from an unregistered congregation in Moscow, now serving three years for holding a service not under the auspices of a registered church.

A typical interruption of a service occurred on September 29, 1985, at Brest, when the police stormed in on 350 members of an unregistered congregation holding a harvest festival service in their tent. First the police used intimidation and insults to frighten the organizers into disbanding the meeting. When they were unsuccessful they resorted to using loudspeakers and sirens. Finally they moved in to break the tent down around the people, overturning tables, smashing benches, and confiscating the public address equipment. Many arrests were made, which led to heavy fines.

The crime of "deliberately inventing falsehoods" is also very easy for an unregistered believer to commit. Pastor Nikolai Baturin, secretary of the Council of Unregistered Baptist Churches, was charged with this offense while in prison and received his seventh prison sentence at a trial held before he had completed his sixth prison term. At this trial the presiding judge made the following statement:

> Under the influence of extremist dogma, Baturin has been occupied in systematically spreading in speech and in writing deliberate falsehoods that defame the Soviet state and

social order. The accused has repeatedly slandered the Soviet press and the internal and external policies of the Communist Party of the USSR in personal conversations with prisoners. He has exerted a religious influence on prisoners and formed illegal contacts outside the camp. He has received forbidden literature published by the Council of Evangelical Baptist Churches [the unregistered Baptist fellowship], which defames the state and social order. He has produced manuscripts of slanderous content that present Soviet legislation on religious affairs in a negative light and has passed them out of the camp by illegal channels. He has had them printed on the prohibited presses of the council of churches. He has spread this slanderous literature among the prisoners.

Under the regulations governing religious groups, believers are forbidden to organize meetings for children and young people, and young people must not be allowed to attend services. They certainly may not be baptized and admitted to church membership. Many of the unregistered Baptists who serve prison sentences do so because they have violated the prohibition of children's work. Three such believers from Mozdok are Natalya Chervyakova, Dina Shvetsova, and Anna Shvetsova, aged thirty-three, twenty-five, and twenty-three respectively. They were found to be in possession of literature that was "intended to entice juveniles to religious activities."

At their trial, State Prosecutor Filippova revealed the attitude of the authorities in her address to the court. She stated that the case was unusual since it was not thieves or murderers in the dock, but those who had committed crimes against the Soviet people. They had been involved in the secret printing and distribution of literature in which the fatherland was slandered. Prosecutor Filippova said:

> The accused are guilty of the most serious crimes—luring children of young age to sects, and this is a criminal act. They have committed an attack on the lives of helpless children whose understanding has not yet matured. They have poisoned them, teaching them to adore the God they be-

lieve in and to pray to Him with tears, and to sing hymns
such as

> "Flow tears of full repentance,
> Weep, O heart, with longing."

What are they inviting these children to? To fun or
happiness? On the contrary, they instill fear into them, fear
of the most terrible judgment of a God. They teach them
the words—"Behold, I come soon!" As a result the children
risk everything out of fear, and refuse to join the Pioneers
and the Komsomol. They torture themselves in services of
worship, as witnesses have told, and sometimes before the
end of the service they run out of the hot, humid room into
the fresh air, with wet hair and dampened clothing which
damages their health. Twenty years ago the mother of Natalya Chervyakova sat in this dock. She was sentenced for
the same offense—the enticement of young children—and
now her daughter is following in her footsteps. I ask the
court, in the name of all Soviet mothers, to punish most severely these modern-day criminals.

To involve children in either worship or regular family
devotions is a heinous crime in the USSR, and many more
examples could be given of the great danger that Christian
parents and Sunday school workers face. Here is a typical indictment brought against those who organize Sunday school
work, which sent three men from Yoshkar-Ola to jail:

> As organizers and preachers from an unregistered church,
> Chengeterov, Nikolayev and Abramov have led prayer
> meetings with the involvement of children of preschool and
> school-going age. . . . Children have taken an active part in
> their services, reciting poems and singing hymns. The ac-
> cused employed illegally produced spiritual literature for re-
> ligious instruction. . . . Under the leadership of the accused
> a children's choir sang at services. . . . Through their
> preaching they imbued children with the spirit of disrespect
> toward legislation on religious observances, inciting them to
> exhibit a negative attitude towards the Soviet state and its
> social order.

The crime of printing Bibles and other Christian literature is always severely punished, as will be seen in chapter 6. But the distribution of such literature is also a grave offense, and many believers are at present in concentration camps for having helped in this work.

Eduard Evert and Ivan Tkachenko from Makinsk (in northern Kazakhstan) are examples. Eduard had been released from a former prison sentence for only nine months when he was caught along with Ivan carrying eight hundred copies of the New Testament and two hundred copies of the magazine *Herald of Truth* in their Shliguli car in July 1984. Both car and contents were confiscated and the men's homes searched. Eleven days afterwards the two men failed to arrive home after work, and their families discovered that they had been arrested and taken to another town to await trial. Eduard, aged thirty-five and married with six children, received a two-and-one-half-year strict regime sentence and Ivan, aged twenty-six, a two-year sentence.

Ivan Kinas from Tokmak was arrested by militia men who carried out a search of his home just as he was about to begin binding Bibles. He was prosecuted on the grounds that it was an illegal craft, and it was also alleged that the materials had been stolen from the state. For such a serious crime, Ivan received a five-year strict regime prison sentence, and his house and other possessions were confiscated.

Numerous unregistered believers have found themselves charged with "willful disobedience" to the authorities and "violent resistance." Even older believers are sometimes deemed to have violent intentions in their "disobedience." Seventy-six-year-old Peter Shokha has a three-year suspended prison sentence standing over him like an ominous shadow. According to the charge, he led an illegal prayer meeting in which a hundred people, including many young people and children, participated. When a militia officer "advised" the people to disperse, Peter Shokha's disinclination was interpreted as "violent resistance against a militia officer."

Countless believers have lost much of their meager incomes on fines for committing the crime of allowing their houses to be used for unregistered church services. Many have eventually gone to prison and lost their homes. The unregistered church at Kishinev is to lose yet another of its meeting places as the result of a court order. For over twelve years services have been held at the home of Nikolai Nikora. In recent years the meetings have taken place in a tent erected on a large plot of ground that is part of Nikolai's property. Militia officers have torn down this tent four times, and the court has now ordered that the house and land be confiscated and that Nikolai and his wife, who are pensioners, move into a single room in an old people's home. Their land is already being used as a community garbage dump. The supreme court of Moldavia ratified this decision in September 1985.

Vladimir Protsenko allowed his home in a Leningrad suburb to be used for meetings by the eighty members of an unregistered congregation. It led him to a three-year prison sentence and the confiscation of his home. His invalid wife and children have been moved into rented rooms. At Rostov-on-Don the authorities apparently did not trouble to get a court order to deprive Grigori Bublik of his house, which was regularly used for meetings. It was burned down. The responsibility pointed towards the authorities when a fire engine arrived without water or other means of dealing with the blaze.

The crime of vagrancy is invariably alleged against pastors and others who have been released from employment to operate underground and are supported by the churches. They are charged with "systematic vagrancy," as Grigori Kostyuchenko was when he was arrested for the fifth time. His family wrote, "Our father is accused of vagrancy because he does not do any productive work. He has been freed from work by the church in connection with his ministry. The church has accepted responsibility for his family."

When Pastor Peter Peters was rearrested in 1984, he was also accused of systematic vagrancy but it was nothing new for him. His previous prison sentence had been given for "not having been occupied with any work useful to society, but having led a parasitic life."

When Vasili Ryzhuk, aged seventy, returned home after his fourth imprisonment, he was not allowed to have an employment card. There is no social security support for the unemployed, and it became obvious that the authorities intended to charge him after a few months as a malingerer and parasite. He was arrested and released pending further charges. Then he was arrested again in Moscow, but under circumstances that are not clear, he regained his freedom and went underground to serve the churches.

This book is filled with examples of believers from unregistered churches who have been arrested and punished for supposedly criminal activities. Apart from the longer sentences in concentration camps, there has been a staggering number of short detention sentences meted out to unregistered church members. A short sentence means ten to fifteen days spent in labor gangs and overcrowded prisons. This form of intimidation is now so commonplace for unregistered congregations that the following examples will be totally inadequate for conveying the scale on which it is employed.

Believers from the town of Chuguyev went through an outburst of short prison terms in 1984. They wrote:

> Our reverent and orderly services are broken up by the militia, Christian literature is taken from believers, and they are punished with fines and subjected to ten to fifteen days detention. Two of our members have been fined and detained for fifteen days several times, and one is currently under threat of trial on the standard charge of disobedience to the authorities.

Believers in Gorki were gathered on Good Friday 1984 to focus their thoughts on the sufferings of Christ. The service had scarcely begun when militia officers appeared and ordered the congregation to disperse immediately. Although they obeyed the order, the names of all present were noted, and the men were driven to the militia headquarters. Five of the men were sentenced to fifteen days detention, seventy-three-year-old Ivan Rybakov among them.

The militia and KGB have various ways of apprehending believers. Frequently they are picked up at work. Others will be traveling on a long journey, visiting other believers, attending a special service, perhaps engaged in some special spiritual service, when they will find themselves intercepted at bus or train stations or as they leave a plane. A believer who maintains a good testimony can never be sure if he or she will return home.

The violent breaking up of meetings is a form of punishment that is relentlessly inflicted upon unregistered congregations. Fines have also become commonplace for the members of churches. In a single year members of the small congregation in the town of Orel had to pay fines totaling 9,495 rubles, equivalent to $12,650.

Another form of punishment is the sudden house search. At any time, without warning, police and KGB officials may burst into the house of an active believer and turn everything upside down. For hours they will sift through the contents of every room and every drawer. They invariably find Christian literature, cassettes, hymnbooks, photographs, or letters, which they confiscate. Usually this leads to a heavy fine upon occupants of the house. A statistic from a recent *Prisoner Bulletin* (from the Council of Prisoners' Relatives) provides an insight into the harassment of an unregistered congregation in the Belgorod area. During a single day in August 1984 no less than thirty homes were subjected to traumatic house searches. The Azarov family from Belgorod wrote the following description of the search.

> The leaders of the house search take away everything they want, not merely those items specified in the search warrant. We, the occupants, sit there like prisoners. Alongside

the militia men whose names we know, there are a number of strangers involved in the search. The investigators rush in and out. They take pictures off the walls and examine them as if they know what they are looking for. They take the covers off the sofa, churn through the beds, empty cupboards onto the floor, seize Bibles, other books, any cash books or receipts, all private letters, and many other items.

During the search of their home, Mrs. Azarova and her daughter-in-law were subjected to a body search. Throughout the proceedings there were constant insults to the family and no opportunity to debase them was lost. The father of the family, Mikhail, was in a remand prison at the time because he had arranged a homecoming service for his son from compulsory military service. Mikhail was subsequently sent to a concentration camp for five years, where he has been put to work felling trees, despite the fact that he suffers from a serious heart condition.

Why do such believers suffer? They do not address themselves to political themes as political dissidents. They do not oppose the government. They are in no sense law-breaking, unruly, riotous citizens. Yet in the USSR they are criminals simply because they cannot hide their spiritual light under a bushel and accept the crippling restrictions of state control in the operation of their church life—restrictions that are acknowledged by the authorities to be designed to eventually eliminate faith in God.

5
Twelve Brave Women

The Council of Prisoners' Relatives is an organization of twelve remarkable and courageous women who are mainly the wives and mothers of unregistered Baptist prisoners. All have themselves experienced arrest and interrogation and suffer continuous surveillance, house searches, body searches, and similar harassment.

Last year Ulyana Germanyuk was arrested and sentenced to three years imprisonment following house searches at her home. (Her story is told in chapter 8.) Serafima Yudintseva was also arrested and given a two-year deferred sentence. That is not the same as a suspended sentence, because Mrs. Yudintseva must serve that sentence irrespective of whether she commits any further offenses. The present leader of the council, Alexandra Kozorezova, has been forced to go into hiding because it became obvious that she was about to be arrested. She already has a three-year suspended sentence, and any further proceedings will lead to imprisonment.

These women publish the details of arrests, sentences, fines, beatings, house searches, and forced admissions into psychiatric hospitals for the unregistered churches. They also organize relief to prisoners' families and coordinate the work of pleading to the authorities on behalf of prisoners who are known to be suffering ill-treatment.

The council has been in existence for more than twenty-two years, a clear indication of the sustaining presence of God when one considers how many human rights groups have been successfully torn apart by the authorities. Andrei Sakharov's Committee for Human Rights is only one of a number of courageous efforts on the part of intellectual dissidents to draw attention to various aspects of persecution in the USSR, but like all others, including Alexander Solzhenitsyn's relief fund for political prisoners set up in 1974, it has suffered speedy dismantling at the hands of the KGB.

No group has survived like that of the all-woman Council of Prisoners' Relatives of Evangelical Baptist Churches. Since its formation in 1964, it has published more than 130 issues of its substantial information magazine called the *Prisoner Bulletin*. The aim of this magazine is not to express a political point of view or to make political demands. Its function is to inform believers in the Soviet Union and elsewhere about those who are suffering persecution, call believers to prayer, and relieve the families of sufferers, for there is no state support for the dependents of criminals in Russia.

As we have mentioned already, the movement of unregistered Baptist churches began in 1961 when a large number of registered congregations affiliated to the officially permitted Baptist denomination took a stand against the oppressive restrictions placed upon such registered churches and founded their own fellowship. Immediately many of their pastors were arrested, and within three years more than one hundred key preachers and workers were in concentration camps.

Dependent families were left destitute, often homeless, and prisoners sent to camps so far away from their families that, for many, visits simply could not be afforded. To make matters worse, the prisoners were subjected to terrible ill-treatment in their labor camps. The response of the remaining pastors of the unregistered churches was to hold a secret conference, inviting all the prisoners' relatives to lay their problem before the Lord in prayer. The result was the formation of the Council of Prisoners' Relatives, which was founded upon four basic rules:

1. The council would provide a continuous information service to the churches about imprisoned believers from the fellowship and also about other forms of persecution, such as children being taken away from parents.
2. The council would make representation to the government on behalf of all Baptist prisoners, appealing for a review of their cases and their release, and also on behalf of children taken from believing homes.
3. The council would collect all details and keep an accurate record of all prisoners and their location.
4. The council would consist only of members of Evangelical Baptist (unregistered) Churches having relatives who had been imprisoned for the Word of God. These members would be elected by periodic conferences of prisoners' relatives.

From its inception the council received total cooperation from all unregistered churches. Details of arrests and sentences were promptly provided, together with details of the needs of dependents. One significant feature of the founding conference was an appeal that was addressed to all believers in these words: "This conference regards it as vital to remind believers that they should not harbor any hostility toward their persecutors, but that they should pray for those who persecute and insult them according to Matthew 5:44."

Over the years the council has provided an amazing news service to unregistered churches and to believers in other countries, and although its members have paid a heavy price, their work has been the means of stirring up earnest and informed prayer throughout the world. Because of this prayer, and because the attention of countless believers has been focused upon the plight of individual prisoners, and also because so many letters and telegrams have been sent to prisoners at their camps, the cruelties of these camps have frequently been ameliorated. Often desperately sick believers have been transferred to prison hospitals, whereas without all the prayer and interest, they would undoubtedly have been left to die. The council has also played a role in distributing relief to needy families, paying for visits, meeting the cost of fines, and so forth.

The *Prisoner Bulletin* magazine, which is regularly distributed, includes many accounts of persecution from local congregations, some of these being included in this book. The articles are always signed; information is never given without the name and address of the writer, who is prepared to stand behind the report.

The activities of the council are regarded as serious criminal offenses. The spreading of information about persecuted Christians and the distribution of material aid to prisoners' families is clearly a great evil in the eyes of the authorities. The women who serve on the council must therefore come to terms with constant surveillance by the KGB. Even at home they must never forget that walls have ears. When they leave home to attend a meeting, they must somehow shake off the officers who will be following them. Sometimes one of the women will not succeed, and their meeting will be traced and roughly interrupted. On one occasion six women were arrested and held for fifteen days. As a result of that meeting Lydiya Bondar received a sentence of three years in prison. Upon her release last year she found that the authorities had not finished with her, for they barred her from returning to her hometown and forced her to live in a town where she had no connections, one thousand miles to the north.

Among more recent prisoners are two older women, Alevtina Panfilova and Valentina Kokurina. They were never members of the council but went to prison because they helped to print and distribute its magazine. Lyubov Skvortsova, at twenty-four years of age, went to prison for the same reason.

As numerous human rights groups arise and disappear, how much longer can the Council of Prisoners' Relatives survive? So far it has outlived them all, published vastly more, and cared for a great number of people. Yet the members of this council are unknown wives and mothers, none of whom has the advantage of high social or academic standing. Clearly their success and survival is because of the keeping power of the Lord and His blessing upon their efforts.

In the following pages several of the council's members —past and present—tell us a little about themselves, such as how they came to know the Lord, how they feel about separation from their loved ones, or how they are sustained and helped to carry on their vital and dangerous ministry.

ALEXANDRA KOZOREZOVA

Alexandra Kozorezova has led the Council of Prisoners' Relatives since 1979. She first became a prisoner's relative in 1966 when her husband, Pastor Alexei Kozorezov, was imprisoned. He has received three further terms of imprisonment since then, the last being an eighteen-month sentence imposed just as he was about to be released from prison at the end of 1983.

Mrs. Kozorezova here tells of how she was arrested in 1981 shortly after her husband suffered his second arrest following a massive search.

ALEXANDRA'S STORY

From just before his arrest a strange, tense atmosphere enveloped me, for I realized that I could be arrested any moment. So that I could continue doing the work I carried out for the Council of Prisoners' Relatives (and on the advice of the church members) I left home and went into temporary hiding with my three-year-old son. My nine other children stayed behind with their grandmother.

Believers in the Soviet Union and overseas supported our family at that time by prayer and also with letters and appeals to the authorities. On February 25, 1981, I was arrested in Belgorod and taken under guard to Voroshilovgrad. My trial was set for March 24. Twice it was altered, and it finally took place on August 20-21 in the Voroshilovgrad District Court.

During the trial the magistrates and the KGB officials were highly agitated, and it soon emerged that they were very apprehensive that foreign news correspondents might attend. I was given a suspended three-year prison sentence.

I praise the Lord for the wonderful paths along which He guides me. I thank Him for the great service that He has entrusted to me, one of the very least among His children. I do it with great joy and am glad that I can share in the suffering of my people, my friends, my brethren, and my sisters. I would like to be a tool in His hands always, a vessel fit to be used for all that He wants. To Him, my Lord Jesus Christ, be honor, glory, and thanksgiving!

*   *   *

At the time of her trial Mrs. Kozorezova petitioned the authorities in these words:

> Our children need both their father and mother. Seven of them are below the age of seventeen, and one, an eighteen year old, is an invalid. (He has had polio since childhood and has no use of his arms and legs. He needs the constant attention of his mother.) I declare once again that my work with the Council of Prisoners' Relatives, which exists because Christians are persecuted and imprisoned for their faithfulness to God, is no crime. Prompted by the unified goal of easing the situation of Christians in the Soviet Union, standing up for the rights which, by your own declaration before world public opinion, are theirs, and having a part, even though it be small, in the suffering of God's people, I am convinced that this work was entrusted to me by God and is directed by Him alone and am prepared with His help to carry on this commission until my last breath.

Mrs. Kozorezova was eventually forced to go underground in June 1985 when it was clear that her rearrest was imminent. But the attention of the authorities then focused upon her husband, Alexei, for his imprisonment would leave the youngest children without parents and render them subject to a state care order.

Alexei was arrested during a harvest thanksgiving service in November 1985 and given a caution, as he was already under an order banning him from attending any meetings of his unregistered church. He was clearly told that the next offense would take him back to prison. For all that this couple have accomplished to help prisoners a price has to be paid, and as this book goes to press, moves by the KGB to extinguish their efforts and administer vengeance are well advanced.

ANTONINA SENKEVICH

Antonina Senkevich tells of her conversion and how she came to serve on the Council of Prisoners' Relatives.

ANTONINA'S STORY

I was born in St. Petersburg, now Leningrad. My father was Polish and a Roman Catholic, and my mother Russian, belonging to the Orthodox Church. When I was six we moved to Grodno in Poland where I received my schooling. My father saw to it that I was brought up in the spirit of Polish nationalism. The person of Jesus caught my attention from my earliest childhood, and I often argued with my religious-knowledge teachers about the worship of Mary, for I thought that it took glory from Christ. My parents each taught me to pray according to their own denominational beliefs, so I learned to pray in both Polish and Russian. Partly under pressure from my Polish environment, and partly because I was seeking to find God, I joined the Catholic Church just before the war. From that moment my mother became very cruel to me.

There was also a Baptist connection in my family, for my cousin who lived next door was a Baptist believer. My father often had violent arguments with her. Soon after I joined the Catholic Church, a Baptist preacher named Ilya Senkevich came to Grodno, having just completed studies at a Bible college, and began to preach in my cousin's church. Very soon the outbreak of war restricted his work. In the very first year of the war my father died at the front, and my brother was taken prisoner by the Germans. I naturally drew closer to my cousin and went next door to see her much more often.

Then in 1941 Ilya Senkevich lost his home and became a tenant in my cousin's house. From that time I frequently heard God's Word explained in that house, but it did not move me for a long time. However, three years later, when Ilya Senkevich was arrested for refusing to enlist for military service, I acquired my own Polish Bible and drew closer to the Baptists.

Another three years went by before I truly found Christ as my own personal Savior. Then my attendance at the Baptist services became marked by keen enthusiasm. My mother reacted angrily and intimidated me so much that after a year I gave up my attendance. I became a "nighttime" reader of God's Word and often tried to witness to my mother. But it was seven years before I made a stand and resumed my attendance at the meetings, eventually being baptized and received into fellowship.

After the war, Grodno came under Soviet rule, and my brother invited us to emigrate and join him in Poland. To do so would have created many difficulties because he was antagonistic towards my Baptist affiliation. I prayed a great deal for guidance, and then the guidance came. Pastor Ilya Senkevich had been away from Grodno for seven years, but about this time he came to visit his old congregation and stayed with my cousin's family. I met him often, and when he asked for my hand in marriage the problem of whether I should emigrate to Poland was solved. We were married in 1957, and I went to serve the Lord with him in the town of Slonim.

In 1961 we found out about the action group and its concern for renewal in the Baptist churches, and we immediately joined it. Ilya was later ordained as a preacher among these churches. Because of his zeal as a pastor he was arrested in 1972 and sentenced to five years imprisonment. After my husband's arrest I was invited to serve on the Council of Prisoners' Relatives. Right from the start it was a great joy to me to share the zealous efforts of my sisters in the Lord. My husband was released from prison in 1975, but I am happy to be able to continue serving on the Council of Prisoners' Relatives and will employ all the strength that the Lord gives me in serving Him and my fellow laborers.

VERA KHOREVA

Vera Khoreva is the wife of imprisoned Soviet Baptist leader Pastor Mikhail Khorev, who recently had a five-year sentence, his third prison term, extended by two years to end in 1987. Pastor Khorev is pastor of the unregistered Baptist congregation at Kishinev and received the five-year sentence for conducting wedding services and worship meetings. He was also ordered to forfeit his home and all private possessions, leaving his family destitute. Pastor Khorev is known to be in very poor health and is almost blind, yet as recently as the end of 1984 he was kept for over three months in a punishment block at Omsk prison. He is a member of the Council of Unregistered Baptist Churches. In the following, Mrs. Khoreva summarizes their lives.

VERA'S STORY

I was born in 1936 near Kishinev, in what was then the Rumanian area of Moldavia. There were eleven of us in the family, and our parents were sound, evangelical Christians. My father served as a church deacon for fifty years. As children, at school we received religious instruction from Orthodox priests who, supported by the authorities, oppressed the nonorthodox believers.

During the war my father was arrested because he refused to accept the orthodox faith. The police searched our home and threw a Bible and other Christian books into the burning oven while we all watched. After Moldavia was absorbed into the USSR in 1945, I continued my education in the

Soviet schools. I received medical training to be an army surgeon and went on to the University of Kishinev for advanced training.

At the university it was soon known that I had believing parents, and since I was not a member of the Communist Youth Organization I was exposed to many difficult trials. But these trials led me to seek and find the Lord for myself, and the Lord wonderfully helped me through all my difficulties. After my conversion I became actively involved in the work of my church's youth group.

Despite much opposition and hostility I graduated successfully from the university in 1959 and was engaged as a doctor with the Russian railways. In 1961 I married Mikhail Khorev, who was then responsible for the young people's work in his church. The year following our marriage he was appointed to undertake service for the whole constituency of churches, which meant much traveling for him. Then, in 1963, under threat of impending arrest, he was forced to go underground to carry out the work entrusted to him. On May 19, 1966, my husband and Pastor Georgi Vins visited the Central Committee of the Communist Party of the Soviet Union to make inquiries concerning the fate of a five hundred-strong delegation of believers—all of whom had been arrested two days earlier. Both men were themselves arrested as they left the Central Committee building.

Georgi Vins was sentenced to three years imprisonment, and my husband received two-and-one-half years. Soon after his release from that prison term my husband was arrested again and sent back to the concentration camp for another three years. In 1980 he was arrested for the third time and sentenced to five years imprisonment together with confiscation of all his private property. [This term is now extended to 1987.]

We have three sons: Ivan, born in 1962, Pavel, born in 1963, and Veniamin, born in 1965. All three have come to know the Lord. The upbringing of the boys lay almost exclusively on my shoulders, because in the twenty years of our marriage my husband has had to live underground for about five years, and so could only come home occasionally and secretly.

For the remainder of the time when he was not in prison, his service to the churches around the land took him away from home considerably. In the past ten years our home has been searched eight times, and on every occasion all spiritual literature has been confiscated. Once our cassette recorder, cassettes, and all the money we had was taken from us.

Throughout all our trials the Lord has granted our family many blessings, and looking back over the years I can truly repeat the words of the psalmist David, "The lines are fallen unto me in pleasant places. . . . Blessed are they which are persecuted for righteousness' sake" [Psalm 16:6; Matthew 5:10].

Lyubov Rumachik

Lyubov Rumachik's husband, Pyotr, is also an imprisoned pastor and a member of the Council of Unregistered Baptist Churches. Their church at Dedovsk has been continuously persecuted since its formation, and news still comes through regularly of meetings being broken up with much brutality and members' homes being searched. Pastor Rumachik's own testimony appears in chapter 15. Here Mrs. Rumachik, who makes a great contribution to the work of the Council of Prisoners' Relatives, responds to a request to say something about herself.

lyubov's story

I was born into a believing family from Dedovsk near Moscow and attended services from earliest childhood. I was converted at the age of seventeen but could not be baptized because the registered Baptist church in Moscow, to which my parents then belonged, complied with the regulations forbidding the baptism of anyone under thirty years of age.

In 1955 I married Pyotr Rumachik and began to attend the church in Dedovsk, which had been founded the previous year and where I was baptized. Our new church grew continuously and by 1961 had about two hundred members. However, because it was not registered it was exposed to severe persecution. Several of the church's key workers including my husband were arrested and exiled to Siberia for five years in 1961. The following year our two children and I went to be with him in exile. Although we received many threats we continued to hold meetings in our house there, and the Lord preserved us in a wonderful way. Then, after our period of exile, we returned to Dedovsk.

Soon after our return I attended a meeting of all the women whose husbands were being persecuted. At that meeting, Lydia Vins emphasized how important it was to the whole group of churches that the women should not stand in the way of their husbands if the Lord wanted to use them in His service. She challenged us all about our readiness to yield our men for the work of the ministry. The Holy Spirit then showed me clearly that in no circumstance should I put myself in his way. As it turned out, my husband was ordained as an evangelist that very year.

In 1967 the authorities commenced proceedings against him, and he was forced to go underground. But he was quickly found and arrested, although I was not informed of that. It was only when our house was entered with a search warrant that I realized he had been apprehended. I traveled to Voronezh where he was being held to take him food and warm clothing. He was sentenced to three years imprisonment. In January 1969, after serving only half of his sentence, Pyotr was released under a general amnesty. But in little over a year he was arrested again and sentenced to three years strict regime, which he served in a concentration camp in the Ural district. Shortly after the sentencing I visited him there for the first time with our two-month-old baby.

Not long after I became an active member of the Council of Prisoners' Relatives in 1968, I was summoned to Moscow by the KGB and threatened in these terms: "If you sign a petition of the Council of Prisoners' Relatives ever again, you will end up where your husband is." I was also summoned before the authorities in Dedovsk where I was threatened with the removal of my parental rights.

The trials of our faith were especially difficult in 1972. Pyotr was in captivity, I was under threat of arrest, and our eldest daughter, scarcely sixteen years old, died of a kidney disease. Due to the appalling and hostile publicity, people would point the finger at me in the street and say, "She sacrificed her daughter to her God."

But we remained certain of God's love to us and equally certain that our daughter had gone home to the Lord. In 1973 Pyotr was released, but he was arrested again in February 1974 and punished with a further three years in strict regime concentration camps. Then followed three years of tense "freedom." In August 1980 he was arrested for the fifth time and sentenced to five years in a concentration camp.

We have six children aged between ten and twenty-six years. The older three are church members and are actively involved in the work of our local church.

*   *   *

Pastor Rumachik's testimony, and the record of his defense before the court when he was last sentenced, appear in chapter 15. Mrs. Rumachik has lived through five years of great burdens while her husband has been subjected to blatant measures to break his health in a camp in far eastern Siberia. In one letter he wrote, "God alone knows what this new year will bring for me. It seems to me that a meeting with Him will take place. I feel rather as Nikolai Khmara did. Please pray for me. Until we meet again, probably in Canaan.

That reference to a martyred believer, coupled with the sentiments about death, suggested that he was receiving hideously brutal treatment. No visitor was allowed to see him for nearly a year after that letter. A once robust and vigorous man has now been reduced to a barely recognizable semi-invalid with a serious heart condition. Furthermore, as this book goes to press he had not been released at the conclusion of his sentence, and new charges have been brought against him. It is probable that he will suffer a new sentence in accordance with the policy that the authorities seem to have adopted to keep senior Baptist preachers away from their churches.

Serafima Yudintseva

We have already mentioned Serafima Yudintseva, who is the first member of the council to receive a peculiarly cruel form of punishment—a deferred or postponed prison sentence. She must begin her two-and-one-half year term in 1987. Mrs. Yudintseva was tried in the town of Khartsyzsk on a charge of "organizing or taking part in group activities that disrupt public order" and also with "having influenced other believers not to register their churches and recognize the laws on religious observance."

The trial was presided over by Judge Burlaka, who made mention of the fact that Mrs. Yudintseva was a member of the Council of Prisoners' Relatives, but that fact was clearly the real reason she was brought to trial. Most of the witnesses were militia officers.

Vasili and Serafima Yudintsev were married in 1957 and supported the unregistered Baptist movement from its inception in 1961. Vasili was first arrested in 1966, serving three years for his part in leading the worship of an unregistered church and for instructing his children in the faith. Soon after that, Serafima began to help the Council of Prisoners' Relatives. Since then she has endured constant spying and many house searches.

After his release from prison, Vasili became a lay pastor but was eventually forced to go underground to continue his work for the churches. In 1982 the Yudintsev's eighteen-year-old son, Andrei, was arrested when a harvest festival service was broken up, and sentenced to a harsh three-and-one-half-year prison term, which has recently come to an end.

Serafima continues with the courageous work of the council, but it seems unlikely that the KGB will leave her alone in the period before her sentence begins. She has already been cautioned twice since her trial for alleged breach of her probation order, which forbids her to attend any services or to leave the town of Khartsyzsk. A third infringement will lead to immediate imprisonment.

6
Sofia's Secret Ministry

One of the reasons for the ferocity of the persecution aimed at unregistered Baptists is their amazing achievement in printing and circulating Bibles, magazines, and tracts. Four hundred thousand items were printed during the first ten years of this underground printing ministry despite the complete lack of commercial equipment. Sophisticated but entirely homemade offset-lithography printing presses operate at a chain of secret locations. From time to time a printing unit is found, and its members are given heavy sentences for the crime of producing gospel literature.

The Christian publishing ministry of the unregistered Baptist community is probably the most secret undertaking in the Soviet Union. The ordinary members of that community know little more about its operations than Christians in the West. The names of the secret printers are known only to a very few. When someone suddenly disappears from his or her local church, it may only be known that this person has "gone into the ministry." Nothing more will be known until after the arrest or death of the worker concerned.

Sofia Bocharova, a pioneer in this ministry, went home to the Lord at the age of fifty-one. After eleven years with the printing ministry she became ill with lung cancer. Now her story of devotion can be told. In her youth, Sofia ordered her life to suit herself, as most people do, yet she felt a great emptiness and longed for something better. She was twenty-nine when she came to know the Lord. At the time she worked as a teacher in a nursery school and lived in a hostel in Noginsk, near Moscow. Her roommate was not a believer, but she possessed a New Testament and some other Christian literature that had been given to her by believing relatives. In the evenings this young woman would read aloud from the New Testament to all who cared to listen. As Sofia listened to these readings, the gospel message affected her like a breath of air from heaven. She believed it without doubt as the only saving truth and gave herself to the Savior. They were marvelous evenings for her as she listened with friends to readings from the Bible and other Christian works such as *The Pilgrim's Progress.*

Occasionally they would travel to the meetings of the Baptist church in Moscow, but later they found that a small group of believers met in a nearby town, and they joined with them. That little congregation consisted of elderly believers who were moved to tears at the sight of their five young guests. Sofia's fellow workers at the nursery noticed the transformation in her and asked about the cause of it. Then she told them openly about her conversion and about the joy that she had received. The result was only typical of the experience of believers. Regardless of her conscientious work and her abilities, she was dismissed.

After a short while five more young women were converted in her church, but the influx of young people attracted the attention of the authorities. The elders were summoned and ordered to pay heavy fines. Then the services of worship were disrupted by police. Finally the young people were forced to separate themselves from the church to deliver the old people from the despotism of the authorities.

When, in 1961, the action group was formed among Baptist churches, Sofia was among the courageous band of believers who mastered homemade duplicating techniques to produce appeals to the churches. From her earliest involvement in this work, Sofia distinguished herself by her faithfulness and astounding thoroughness. Anyone acquainted with the kind of duplicating process employed for these early efforts knows how difficult it was to maintain order, cleanliness, and secrecy. Yet Sofia always managed to keep things under control and survived numerous police searches of her home. Many times she experienced the overruling protection of the Lord.

On one occasion it had been arranged for a number of believers to visit Sofia, each with a pack of unprinted paper. Sofia proceeded to duplicate the literature that they were to take away for distribution at a secret meeting the same evening. All went according to plan until the time came for the couriers to leave Sofia's house.

Unfortunately, several neighboring women had settled down for a long chat on a bench immediately outside Sofia's house. The couriers were unable to leave for fear that their carrier bags would arouse the curiosity of these neighbors. For hours the couriers waited while the seemingly endless chatter continued. It was late evening before they could get away. When they eventually arrived at the secret distribution meeting, an anxious hostess greeted them with surprise and relief. "However did you get through?" she asked, "The police have only just left—they have been watching the house all day."

It was in Sofia's house that a small group of believers attempted to design and build the first underground offset press. Their initial task was to find out whether it was possible to achieve a functional printing plate under primitive conditions. Only if this was possible would there be any sense in attempting a homemade machine.

The technical dabblers worked day and night under inadequate conditions and in absolute secrecy to master the technology of homemade plates and printing. They built their experimental machine with whatever materials were available—Sofia's poker, mincer handle, milk cans, and so forth. Sofia looked after all their needs. The interminable experiments of the printers would end by about 4:00 A.M. every morning. But before she left for her day's work at a factory, Sofia would have washed and scrubbed away all evidence of ink and machine oil.

Alongside her involvement in this prolonged, intense, and rigorous project, Sofia continued to personally duplicate a Christian magazine and never missed a meeting of her local church so as not to attract attention to herself. In 1967 she was asked to put herself completely at the disposal of the publishing house. It meant leaving her home and friends and going underground for the Lord.

With Sofia's vital contribution, the publishing house published its remarkable 400,000 items of spiritual literature in ten years. New editions of literature were always made under dangerous circumstances and usually in a rush. Sofia once described her experience in these words: "While working on a new edition I would be filled with a seemingly inexhaustible strength. I would feel no tiredness."

The conditions under which Sofia's printing cell worked were extremely cramped. A small kitchen contained the printing press, numerous reams of paper, and seven or eight workers. At night the equipment would be pushed into corners so that the printers could kneel for prayer and then lie down to sleep on the floor.

In such circumstances who could be concerned about order and cleanliness? Who would expect such exhausted workers to straighten things out? But Sofia, accompanied only by the heavy breathing of sleeping fellow laborers, would always restore order. She would sweep up, clean the machine, wash out their working clothes, and straighten up badly stacked piles of paper. Her sensitivity, carefulness, and thriftiness impressed everyone who had anything to do with her, and she was a caring teacher for newcomers in secret work. She was strict on matters of conduct in the underground, but in a reasoning, persuasive, and pleading manner.

In her twelfth year with the press Sofia became very ill,

and in a secret medical examination it was diagnosed as cancer. Her friends tried to persuade her to give up service in the underground, but she was convinced that she should continue working for the Lord for as long as she was able. When it became clear to Sofia that she did not have long to live, she was filled with peaceful joy.

"The world does not matter for me any longer," she said. "All around gardens are blossoming and giving off sweet scent, but these earthly pleasures do not seem significant any more. My soul no longer belongs here and I begin to feel a foretaste of heavenly things. I am just waiting to meet my Lord."

Sofia is now with the Lord, and this report on her service cannot harm her. But for the reader it offers a glimpse of the life of the secret printers. It is a very demanding and dangerous ministry, and those who engage in it sacrifice comfort, fellowship, and often health and liberty. But the fruit of their work is seen in the quantities of spiritual literature that Soviet believers have received.

At the end of October 1985, an underground press fell into the hands of the KGB at Beltsy, Moldavia. At the time of the raid, six workers were preparing to print New Testaments in Moldavian. A huge quantity of paper—five tons—stood near the machine, half of it already printed. Beltsy was the sixth secret Baptist press to be discovered since 1974, when a unit was uncovered in Latvia. That was followed by the discovery of a press at Ivan-Gorod (near Leningrad) in 1977. Then presses were found at Dnepropetrovsk and Krasnodar in 1980. At the end of 1984 another was found at Issyk, near Alma-Ata. In addition to these presses, the KGB have also succeeded in finding a film and printing plate processing laboratory and several bookbinding workshops.

The workers arrested in Beltsy were chiefly women, including two in their early twenties. They all face long, strict regime prison sentences, which is the rule with those caught operating in the secret publishing house.

When the authorities strike, they move suddenly and effectively. In November 1984, a considerable force of militia surrounded house 26a on Uroshaynaya Street in the town of Issyk, Alma-Ata. They entered the home of Yegor Wolf to find three tons of unprinted paper, a homemade printing press, and a quantity of printed Bibles awaiting binding. Two motor-trucks were required to remove all the printing material, and Yegor Wolf was arrested immediately. As the officers allowed the four children to say good-bye to their father, one said, ''Well, children, say good-bye for five years!'' The following day the home of Yegor's brother Andrei was also raided, and a further three tons of paper was found and confiscated. Andrei was also arrested.

The discovery of such units is a serious blow to the secret publishing operation of the fellowship of unregistered Baptists who supply Bibles and other literature not only for their own huge constituency of churches but for believers in many other churches also. The secret printers work under extremely difficult circumstances, but their output has been of incalculable value. At the beginning of the 1960s, believers in the USSR had virtually no Bibles and no Christian literature. Bibles were copied by hand. Because of the secret printers that is no longer necessary, for they are now better supplied and have Bibles and Testaments in over ten languages. There are also enough hymnbooks. Still, the secret printers have by no means reached their target, which is to provide sufficient Bibles, tracts, and other items of literature to supply to all who need and want them.

In recent years it was announced by one prominent Bible society in Britain that ten thousand Bibles had been imported into Russia with official sanction. Experience demonstrates that very few of these Bibles reach a worthy destination, apart from the fact that this is a very small amount for the thousands of congregations spread across the USSR.

It is probable that the occasional importing of a small consignment of Bibles is allowed purely for propaganda reasons.

The authorities undoubtedly seek to counteract the publicity given to persecuted Baptists and their great need of secret printing units. After all, the same authorities still relentlessly hunt down those who print and distribute Bibles secretly. The work of the secret printers is as vital as ever and highly dangerous.

7
A Narrative of Prison Violence

Vladimir Rytikov, arrested with Galina Vilchinskaya when they were both twenty-one, described in chapter 3 how they were intercepted by the police while helping his father take forty children home after a summer camp for the children of prisoners. While in an interrogation prison a KGB major threatened him in these words: "I suppose you want to become a hero like Ivan Moiseyev. Very well, we'll help you!" Ivan Moiseyev was a young believer who died at the hands of the Soviet prison authorities in 1972.

Vladimir wrote a long report of his prison experiences as soon as he was released, giving another insight into the mixture of subtlety and brutality that even the young believers must expect to have directed against them.

VLADIMIR'S STORY

One day they let into my cell block a man with long hair and a beard. Soon he came over to me, sat on my bunk, and asked simply, "Believer?" When I told him of my trust in the Lord he began to speak about the Bible, showing how very well he knew it. I instinctively felt that this man was probably a KGB plant, for it is a common enough practice for such agents to be sent in to listen to prisoners' conversations and to encourage them to make incriminating remarks. Although there were several other prisoners in my cell, this man remained constantly near to me only. If I began to write anything, he would be looking over my shoulder. If I spoke to another prisoner, he would be standing very close by, listening.

After a month all three of us (my father and Galina also) were moved into the main prison in Lvov. After the usual preliminaries I was taken to a cell containing about twenty prisoners. These immediately surrounded me and asked why I had been arrested. They took an interest in my answers and were kind to me.

Suddenly, however, their behavior changed dramatically. That came about after KGB Major Malyshev, with my investigating magistrate, had spoken to them. He somehow incensed them against me, and when they returned from their interview they shouted at me, saying that they now knew the truth, that I was masquerading as a believer, and that I had been arrested for spreading anti-Soviet literature.

They kept up a bombardment of torment and harassment, taking steps to prevent me from sleeping by throwing cold water over me and by other means. After two months of that I was moved to a smaller cell where again I had to endure the presence of a plant. This time it was a man who said he was a former detective who had been imprisoned for accepting bribes, but it seemed to me that he was now working as an informer for the KGB. His aim was to get something out of me about what we had been doing for our unregistered churches. When he did not succeed he grew increasingly furious, and for six months I was subject to his hostility. He was a very coarse and malicious man who tried every possible way of upsetting me. He even spit into my bowl while I was eating.

Once I was taken to the chief investigating magistrate for the public prosecutor's office in Lvov, whose name was Shevchuk. He demanded that I should sign the statement prepared during my first interrogations. I refused, partly because it contained lies but also because any signature would have constituted a plea of guilty.

Shevchuk became livid at my response. His eyes turned red, and he shouted at me in such a way that he foamed at the

mouth. He snatched the penholder out of the ink pot and began to wave it about wildly, almost as if he intended to stab
my eyes. The Lord gave me courage in my heart, and I was
not afraid. That made Shevchuk more angry than ever, but all
he could do was to send me back to my cell.

Later I was put into a cell for two weeks where smoke
came in through the unglazed window and filled the cell to the
extent that we could not even see the overhead electric light.
We suffered severe headaches and nausea and could get no
response to our complaints. When the investigating magistrate visited he merely said, "Is your head hurting? Then get
ready to be committed to a mental hospital."

Our trial, for which we had had to wait a year, lasted
three days and was mounted rather like a show. Parts of the
trial were even shown on local television. One of the charges
leveled against us was that we had traveled around the
country preaching that children should not be sent to school
because there was little to be gained by it, but that they
should solely be given religious instruction at home.

Since I had completed eleven years schooling and gone
on to a trade college and could make reference to many believing friends in the same position, I was able to show that
this charge was groundless. However, the prosecuting magistrates replied that they had witnesses who said they had
heard us preach such things, although they could not name or
produce those witnesses. We were also charged with distributing anti-Soviet literature, but the prosecutors could not produce evidence for that either.

Despite the unsubstantiated charges, Galina, my father,
and myself were each sentenced to three years imprisonment. The officer in command of the soldiers who were
guarding us came to us after the sentence was passed and
said, "Those magistrates could not prove any one of the
charges against you." Even the non-Christians in court recognized the unreasonable conduct of the public prosecution and
magistrates.

Once back in prison I was ordered to pack my belongings for transportation to a concentration camp. The first stage of the journey to Sverdlovsk took four days, during which time I was greatly uplifted by the Lord and by the believers who were with me. I traveled in the same compartment as Galina and Tamara Bystrova, another convicted believer. In the prison I was put in a cell with Sergei Bublik, another convicted prisoner from our brotherhood. What a joy that was. We embraced each other like brothers and wept for joy at seeing each other again. How we thanked the Lord for His wonderful leading! We spent four great days together in that cell.

Nearly all prisoners who are being transported from the western parts of the country to the eastern, and vice versa, pass through the transit prison in Sverdlovsk. The conditions there are, as far as I know, even worse than those in other transit prisons. When we entered the cell, which was intended for thirty prisoners but was occupied by over a hundred, we were struck by the reddish walls. Our intrigue about this was soon replaced by utter disgust, for as we were arranging ourselves on our bunks along the walls, we discovered that they were covered with innumerable bugs. They climbed up the walls and ceilings and from there dropped onto their human prey. Exhausted by days of sleepless rail travel, we immediately fell into deep sleep, but when we woke we found ourselves bitten all over our bodies.

The joy of having fellowship with Sergei outweighed all the torment of such discomforts. We remembered young people's gatherings, sang our hymns, reflected on the Word of God, and prayed for blessing for the churches and all their ministries. All too soon the command was directed at me, "Go to the cell door with your things!" I was to be sent much further east.

There were fewer bugs in the prison in Novosibirsk, but the cells of the prison in Irkutsk were so overfilled that the majority of their occupants had to stand all the time. From there I was transported on to Talun, my final destination. The whole journey took about a month.

At first I worked in the camp sawmill. In the evenings I was often asked by prisoners to tell them about my faith. Up to one hundred men in the camp heard my testimony, and some were surprised that believers were imprisoned.

After six months I was called into the commandant's office where I was met by KGB Captain Petrov. He asked me to write an appeal in support of the registration of churches. If I would do so, he promised to send me to work on state farms, or even to release me. I declined that offer. Captain Petrov was also interested in the way in which our brotherhood had emerged in 1961. It was, I believe, for my "uncooperative" spirit that I had been moved to Talun. When I arrived I was brought before the head of the prison. I asked him about the reason for my transfer, and he replied, "You did not justify the trust that was placed in you. That is why you were brought here."

The militia sergeant who led me away unlocked a cell, ordered me to go in, and said to the prisoners who were inside, "Is a week long enough for you?" "Yes," they replied. I found myself shut in with three young men. They asked me about my faith and about life in the concentration camp. Then they moved to the tasks that they had probably been given by Captain Petrov. They first tried to persuade me to cooperate with the KGB officer, saying, "Write to him saying that you renounce God, and you will be released from imprisonment. You can then enjoy all you want. You will be given a good flat, and if you should have a son he could even become an astronaut."

They then began to make threats: "We will kill you like a dog today! We will tread you into the concrete of the floor, we will push you so far that you will renounce God!" One of them came at me, kicked me, and said, "Where is your God? I have hurt you, but He did not stand by you! Why did He not hold my foot back?" However, as the days passed threats increased and became even more malicious. Sunday came, and as the situation was becoming acute I decided to spend the day fasting and praying. Very early in the morning the three men began sharpening knives.

I lay on my bunk and prayed that the Lord would make me resolute, and I thought about how the early Christians were martyred. The Lord enabled me to maintain a peaceful demeanor, and their determination to intimidate me was broken. Soon afterwards I was taken out of that cell and put to work in the prison services. Then I was returned to my concentration camp and put in the punishment isolation unit for two weeks. After a further two weeks in ordinary camp quarters, I was locked away again, but on the way to the unit the militia wardens beat me with billy clubs. Then they tried to incite other prisoners against me.

On the morning of my release, after three years of cell life, my mother and other believers met me at the camp gates, and we drove to meet my father who had also just been released from a Siberian prison camp. We then drove together to Krasnodon and went straight to the registration office where we had to obtain new identity cards. Once there, we were shown into a side room to await the arrival of the public prosecutor for Krasnodon and representatives of the head of the militia. They immediately demanded that we should have our church registered, and they threatened that we would be rearrested if registration did not take place. My father said they could imprison him again immediately, for he would not take a single step towards registration. He was told he would certainly be arrested again in due time.

*   *   *

Pastor Pavel Rytikov, Vladimir's father, was rearrested on January 30, 1986, after a brief period in freedom. He is the pastor of the unregistered Baptist church at Krasnodon and has endured strict regime imprisonment several times. His wife, Galina Rytikova, is also well-known to Western readers because of her work with the Council of Prisoners' Relatives. She has had to go into hiding with her three younger children in order to avoid being committed to a psychiatric unit, another method used by the KGB to prevent key Christian workers from carrying on their service.

During an earlier term of imprisonment awaiting trial, Pastor Rytikov was offered the following deal by Major P. Anenko the Kiev KGB and Major M. Drokin of the Voroshilovgrad KGB: "You must agree to collaborate secretly with us, and then you will be given liberty. If you do not agree you will get a five-year sentence, and we will even make your prison term harder."

Pavel Rytikov refused and was sentenced to five years in a closed trial. Once in prison he was repeatedly offered his freedom if only he would agree to become the pastor of a registered congregation and assist the local KGB.

Pastor Rytikov was a member of the Council of the Unregistered Churches when he was arrested in 1979 with his son Vladimir and Galina Vilchinskaya. Throughout that three-year sentence he had the same offer—"Register your church and all will be well! Refuse, and you will soon be back in prison!"

When he was released, he encountered a problem—the authorities did not return his employment card to him. Without that card it was impossible to obtain employment, so Pavel Rytikov applied to the court that had confiscated his card during his trial. They no longer had his file, and no one else seemed inclined to help him. In April 1983, after only seven-and-one-half months of freedom, he was arrested in Stakhanov on a charge of parasitism because he had not been employed since his release from prison. He was duly sentenced to another two years in prison.

In 1985 this Russian pastor returned home again, but for how long? Pavel Rytikov is now fifty-four-years old and has spent a total of ten years in prison. He is under "administrative surveillance" for one year and is not allowed to leave his house between 8:00 P.M. and 8:00 A.M.

Shortly after his release the police forced their way into the Rytikov's home at about 1:00 A.M. and found the whole family gathered together, including Vladimir, newly married, who was visiting with his wife and some friends. Pastor Rytikov was taken to police headquarters where he was fined and warned that he was not allowed to have strangers in his home on the grounds that he would entice them into his beliefs.

An example of the constant pressure upon this family was seen during Easter 1985. On a Saturday evening there was a forceful knock on the door of Vladimir Rytikov's home. His sister Nina was with him at the time, and being familiar with those ominous knocks since early childhood, they did not respond. The militia officers attempted to break down the door. Failing in that they pushed in a window pane in order to force an entry and promptly began to search the house. Soon they smashed open the door of a room where several women visitors were attempting to sleep.

"We have the right to do anything we want!" the captain shouted. They then arrested seven people and took them away. After interrogation Vladimir and his sister Nina were held in the cells, while his wife and four others were allowed to go home. Once in the cells Vladimir was threatened that all kinds of things could happen to him. He could, for example, be killed in a car accident.

When Galina Rytikova heard of her children's arrest she immediately set out for Voroshilovgrad. The next day, when she was in their house, the militia again banged on the door. This time a woman shouted, "Open up, sisters! Open up!" Because no one opened the door, the order was given, "Repeat yesterday's action!"

Once again a window was pushed in and a forced entry made. When they noticed Mrs. Rytikova they demanded to see her papers, arrested her, and took her to the militia headquarters where she was put in the same cell as Nina. After Easter the three were taken to the people's court in Voroshilovgrad. Judge Tolstonosov asked Galina, "Why do you not register your church?" Later, while accusing her of having guests in her house contrary to her husband's probation terms, he said, "If your church was registered, guests would be allowed to come and see you." For failing to open their door they were all fined twenty rubles (a typical weekly wage).

Since Pastor Rytikov's release, the whole family has endured constant interference and surveillance. It was made clear to them that if Rytikov were willing to serve a registered church and accept the authority of the KGB, to work against his brethren, to maintain a pretense of religious freedom, and to cease his evangelistic activity, then he could be protected from arrest and persecution. But Pastor Rytikov would not do this, and is therefore back in custody and facing yet another strict regime prison term.

8

Stepan and Ulyana Keep the Faith

In 1983, Stepan Germanyuk was sentenced to three years in a strict regime prison—his second prison term. He is one of the members of the Council of Unregistered Baptist Churches. At the end of 1985, his wife, Ulyana, was also sentenced to three years in prison. She has been a lay worker for the Council of Prisoners' Relatives for thirteen years.

Ulyana was an eighteen-year-old medical student when she was converted to Christ. She had not grown up in a Christian home, and so the radical change in her life-style was immediately noticed. Her lecturers and fellow students made great efforts to retrieve her from her newfound faith, but when all friendly persuasion failed, they resorted to threats of expulsion. It was under constant harassment that Ulyana battled through to graduate from preliminary medical school.

However, the completion of her training to become a doctor could be no more than a dream. Because of her faith, she was not admitted to the qualifying stage of the course. Ulyana turned her attention to the study of veterinary medicine at an agricultural university, hoping that the authorities would admit her because of the unlikelihood that she would have any harmful religious influence on four-footed patients.

Normally it would be unheard of for a believer to be permitted to complete any higher education course, but somehow Ulyana graduated in veterinary science. Even then the diploma was to be withheld from her until she renounced her belief in God. She did not renounce her belief, but because

Stalin had recently died and believers were being treated leniently for a while, she was given her diploma without meeting the demands of the college authorities.

Ulyana was even given a post as a veterinary surgeon but was given notice fairly quickly because of her Christian convictions. In a second and then a third post she suffered the same fate, and moving to another district did little to help. Soon Ulyana was forced to give up medicine altogether and content herself with working first as a cleaner, then as a stoker, and finally as a watchwoman. Eventually she was designated as unsuitable for that kind of job also and dismissed. Ulyana and Stepan were married just prior to Ulyana qualifying as a vet. They have five children, now between seventeen and twenty-eight years of age.

Stepan was first arrested in 1973 and sentenced to four-and-one-half years imprisonment to be followed by three years exile. The family had lived for years in the knowledge that this could happen any day, any hour. That their fears were not unfounded was confirmed by the words of KGB Major Romashko of Voroshilovgrad shortly before Stepan's arrest. He exclaimed, "You should have served two sentences by now, but here you are—still at home!"

When a believer is arrested, the attitudes of the prisoner's family change in every way. The ordinary things of life lose all significance, and the matter of the prisoner's welfare becomes paramount. To such a family the only time that matters is the length of time that remains until the sentence is up. The family lives in continuous expectation of a letter from the prisoner and in hope of receiving permission to visit.

Ulyana, however, was strengthened by her experience with the work of the Council of Prisoners' Relatives. Having cared for the families of other prisoners and seen how other women bore their trials, she was able to face up to her own circumstances and to prove the help of the Lord.

Stepan's sentence finally came to an end, but that was only the beginning of another phase—a long period of time in exile in a remote community selected by the authorities. Writing to his children, Stepan recorded his journey from the Voroshilovgrad prison.

STEPAN AND ULYANA'S STORY

We were taken to the railway station in black marias, squashed like sardines in a tin. Then, under guard from soldiers with dogs, we were loaded into a railway prisoner-wagon and sent to Kharkov. The wagon was overcrowded for the whole journey with fourteen to sixteen prisoners in every compartment. In Kharkov we were taken for a bath while our clothes were baked to kill the lice. Afterwards we were put into cells.

The other prisoners were very interested in my convictions, and throughout my journey I was able to witness a great deal for my Redeemer. There were many listeners, and few argued. I met an old prisoner who was being sent into exile after a total of thirty-three years imprisonment. He was an embittered man, but when he heard me tell of Christ at some length his heart softened and he said, "I believe in nothing and no one, but this evening as I have listened to you I have been very moved, and I respect what you say."

The last night, before leaving Kharkov for the next stage of our journey, I was put with another prisoner in the prisoners' death cell. It was somewhat uncanny to read the solemn notice: "Went to the sentence of execution," under which were written the dates and names of those executed. On departure from Kharkov we were issued three days' rations (three loaves and one hundred grams* of bacon) and herded once again into the railway prison-wagon. On this trip we passed through Balashevo, Kazan, and through to Sverdlovsk.

The escorting soldiers were not only arrogant but extremely brutal. After a four-day train journey we reached

---

*Approximately three-and-a-half ounces.

Sverdlovsk prison. Here we were given a meal and thrown into a narrow cell without beds or bunks. After receiving rations of three badly-baked loaves and some herring we were put into a large "transit" cell for three days. This cell already held prisoners who had committed crimes ranging from traffic offenses to murder. These pounced on every newcomer who had a bag of food or clothes like vultures on a carcass, taking everything edible as well as other goods.

About twenty men surrounded me and ordered me to open my bag of clothes. It was pointless refusing or complaining to the guards. They took away all that I had prepared for my journey. Some slashed my bag with razor blades and others searched my pockets for money. Everything was taken away, even my folder with letters, envelopes, addresses, and so forth. I was hungry and devoid of possessions.

After the attack the younger prisoners asked me, "Father, what do you think of us?" I answered, "This is a sinful, wicked world, which has sunk as low as it possibly can." And to the question of whether I was angry with them or whether I wanted vengeance, I told them that my Master, Jesus Christ, commanded me to forgive all injuries and not to take revenge.

Once back in the railway wagons our journey took us through Tyumen and Novosibirsk, and eventually we arrived in Krasnoyarsk. Here we were herded into bare cells. Then, after a search, we were transported off to Irkutsk by train. The Irkutsk prison was particularly bad. We were all in a cell with no glass in the windows—the temperature being -15°C (5°F). While the cell contained bunks in three-tier stacks (we had not seen a bed in days), we had no sooner laid ourselves down when we were attacked by hungry bed bugs. The lice-infested mattresses were not exactly attractive. All Soviet prisons have lice; one has to grow used to them.

The following morning we refused our food in protest and were put in another cell. In this cell I met a political prisoner who had spent time in the infamous prison at Vladimir, where he shared a cell with V. Bukovsky. We became friends, but we were soon separated. After the usual frisking we were moved by rail to Khabarovsk, the journey lasting three days. In Khabarovsk prison we were allowed a bath while our clothes were baked. Then we were taken to a cell already holding eighteen prisoners, mostly convicted murderers.

I was given a friendly reception and given a place on one of the lower bunks. I helped many prisoners draft appeals, and during the evenings I told them of the Lord until midnight. All listened very attentively and questioned me constantly, so that I got no rest. The swearers stopped cursing, and the godless became very thoughtful. I lived and spoke with them in this way for thirteen days. Then one night three of us were waked up suddenly and taken to the airport in a black maria. We were handcuffed and sent by air to Nikolayevsk on the Amur.

We remained in the prison there for two days and were then taken in a small plane to our place of exile, the settlement of Chumikan. This settlement is about 1,250 miles away from Khabarovsk. My place of exile is on the coast of the Okhotskion Sea. It is a very barren area with a bleak climate. Strong winds blow throughout the year, and it becomes so cold in winter that it is impossible to get warm. The temperature drops to -30°C (-22°F). Packs of dogs run wild in the settlement. Housing here is very bad. I am now living in the hotel, but it is so cold that my feet are freezing in my boots. I have been allocated work as a storeman in the local department of education.

*   *   *

In April 1978, when Stepan had been in exile for six months, Ulyana and three of their children left the sunny Ukraine to live with him for the rest of his period in Chumikan settlement. For believers there are some advantages to be gained in such remote settlements. Because of the great distance from the cities and the terrible weather conditions, such places suffer from a shortage of skilled and honest workers. In these circumstances exiles often achieve leading positions. By the end of his exile Stepan was not merely a storeman but the chief bookkeeper of a building company in Chumikan. In his own home district his Christian faith would certainly have prevented him from obtaining anything better than manual work. Ulyana also found a job in Chumikan.

The honesty and friendliness of Stepan and Ulyana aroused the respect of the local people, and the family quickly gained a number of friends who would visit their home and listen to their testimony. This could not be kept secret for long, and the day came when militia officers, accompanied by the local public prosecutor, paid them a visit. They searched their house and took away all books and papers in which the name of God was mentioned. Even letters that Stepan had written to his family from the concentration camp—and had thus already been censored by the authorities—were confiscated. He was also threatened with further imprisonment.

Despite this event the family lived in relative peace until the end of their term of exile in Chumikan and returned to the Ukraine, where Ulyana renewed her work with the Council of Prisoners' Relatives. The couple had only been back two years when their home church in Dergadni, near Voroshilovgrad, was severely persecuted. On several occasions the authorities interrupted church services and arrested leading members. During one raid eleven church members were arrested and sentenced to between five and fifteen days in the local prison.

Stepan was arrested and sentenced to fifteen days imprisonment, and within a month that treatment was repeated. Later he was again arrested for taking part in services. Along with the pastor, Stepan was threatened that he would stand trial for a longer sentence if he was caught again.

Such events and threats forced Stepan to move underground to continue his witness, but after nearly two years he was arrested in May 1983 and sentenced to three years in a strict regime concentration camp. For the Lord's sake he has returned to the rigors described in the preceding pages.

Ulyana's arrest in July 1985 came as no surprise because she had been warned that she faced trial for leading in unlawful assemblies, inciting believers to disobey the authorities, and slandering the state. In April 1985 a meeting was broken up of the congregation at Dergachi (in the Kharkov region). Ulyana was arrested along with others and given fifteen days detention. Three months later her house was searched, and it was shortly afterwards, while she was visiting her daughter in the Crimea, that she was apprehended by militia to face the charges that led to a three-year sentence.

Now aged fifty-six, Ulyana has joined the list of godly, middle-aged women who must endure years of inhuman, degrading treatment in Soviet prison camps. As this book goes to press, Ulyana is reported to be dangerously ill in a prison hospital and possibly dying. Together with Stepan she has been a channel of spiritual light and happiness to many and has sacrificed her freedom and possibly her life to minister to the prisoners through her work on the Council of Prisoners' Relatives.

Right: Russia's most wanted Baptist, Pastor Gennadi Kryuchkov, is president of the Council of Unregistered Baptist Churches. Pastor Kryuchkov has lived at home for only eighteen months in the last twenty-five years because of constant police surveillance (chapter 1).

Below: Galina Vilchinskaya, left, shortly after her release from prison in October 1984, sits with her mother. Galina endured cold, hunger, bedbugs, fleas, and lice in prison because she refused to stop her work in the unregistered Baptist churches (chapter 3).

Above: The Council of Prisoner's Relatives risk prison sentences for secretly publishing the *Prisoner Bulletin.* Front row, left to right: Mrs. Vilchinskaya, Alexandra Kozorezova, Serafima Yudintseva, Lyubov Rumachik. Middle row: Mrs. Kryuchkova, Vera Khoreva, Mrs. Kostyuchenko, Galina Rytikova, Antonina Senkevich. Back row: Ulyana Germanyuk, Mrs. Skornyakova, Lydiya Bondar (chapter 5).

Right: Sofia Bocharova, who died at the age of fifty-one, worked underground with the printing press. She survived numerous police searches and was noted for her faithfulness and thoroughness (chapter 6).

Vladimir Rytikov, pictured with his mother,
was told he would be sent to work on a state farm, or even released from
prison, if he would write an appeal in support of the registration of
churches (chapter 7).

Pastor Pavel Rytikov, fifty-four, pictured
shortly after his release from prison in April 1985. Pastor Rytikov is now
back in custody and facing another prison term (chapter 7).

Left: Ulyana Germanyuk, a lay worker for the Council of Prisoner's Relatives for thirteen years, was sentenced to a three-year prison term at the end of 1985. Her husband, Stepan, was previously sentenced to a three-year prison term in 1983 (chapter 8).

Below: Pastor Nikolai Baturin, far right, after his release from prison in 1976. Pastor Baturin has been persecuted for the past thirty-eight years. He was last arrested in 1979, and his present release date is November 1986 (chapter 13).

Left: Pastor Ivan Antonov with his wife, Lina, and children. Pastor Antonov, a former alcoholic doctor, became a believer and has faced imprisonment along with his wife (chapter 14).

Left: Pastor Pyotr Rumachik, fifty-five, faced new prison charges in August 1985. He has already spent more than eleven years in labor camps and exile and five years in prison (chapter 15).

Below: A homecoming service was held on January 26, 1986, celebrating the release of four prisoners: (left to right) Mikhail Azarov (chapter 4), Alexander Bublik, Nikolai Kolbantsev, and Pastor Dmitri Minyakov (chapter 16).

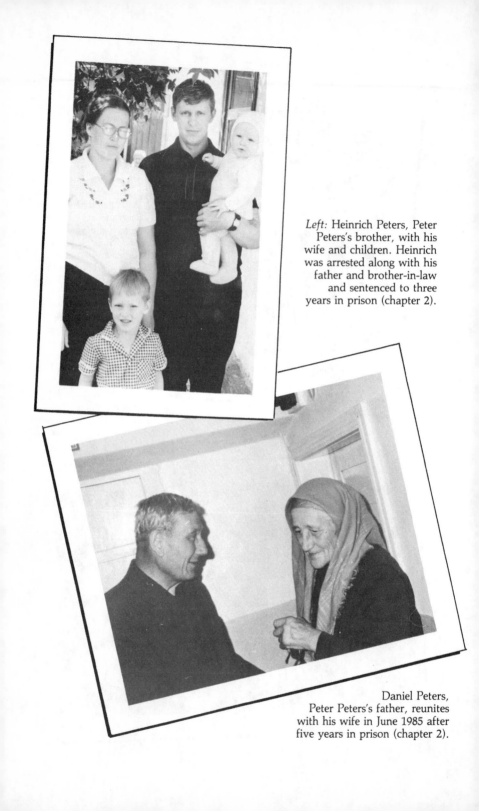

Left: Heinrich Peters, Peter Peters's brother, with his wife and children. Heinrich was arrested along with his father and brother-in-law and sentenced to three years in prison (chapter 2).

Daniel Peters, Peter Peters's father, reunites with his wife in June 1985 after five years in prison (chapter 2).

Above: Anna Shvetsova, left, twenty-three, and her sister Dina, twenty-five, were both imprisoned for possessing literature that was "intended to entice juveniles to religious activities" (chapter 4).

Below: Yevgeni Pushkov, a preacher at an unregistered Baptist church, was sentenced to five years in prison after he refused to register his church with the All-Union Council (chapter 4).

Left: Pastor Mikhail Azarov and his wife in a photograph taken secretly in prison. Pastor Azarov was sent to a concentration camp for five years for arranging a homecoming service for his son returning from military duty (chapter 4).

Alexei Kozorezov, still in prison uniform, with his family after his release in June 1985 (chapter 5).

Vladimir Rytikov and his sister Natasha, center,
wait in the prison waiting room on the day of their double
wedding, April 2, 1985, hoping to see their father, Pastor Pavel
Rytikov. They were denied a visit (chapter 7).

Eduard Evert, pictured with his wife and children,
first went to prison in 1981 for secretly transporting New
Testaments. He is now in prison until 1987 (chapter 9).

Above: Ivan Leven, right, receives a Bible from a group of believers after his release from prison in 1982. Ivan was imprisoned after serving three years in the underground printing ministry (chapter 9).

Left: Anna Chertkova, fifty-eight, has been in a psychiatric unit for fourteen years. She will not be released unless she renounces her faith in God (chapter 10).

Left: Vladimir Khailo, fifty-four, who has been held in a special psychiatric institution since 1980, will be held indefinitely unless he can be "cured" of his religious views (chapter 10).

Right: Vladimir Muzyka refused to take the military oath and was told, "You will never come home alive!" Two months later Vladimir's parents were notified of his death. A postmortem showed severe head injuries as the cause of his death (chapter 11).

Left: Yuri Burda died a few months after he refused to take the military oath. The unit's officer said Yuri died from electrocution but would not allow his parents to see where the alleged accident took place. They have still not received a death certificate (chapter 11).

Below: Sergie Petrenko, far right, visits Victor Orlov in the hospital along with two other friends. In a military unit, Sergie was beaten after he refused to kneel before the sergeant-major and worship him (chapter 11).

Left: Philipp Korniyenko died after a few months in the Soviet armed services. His parents were told he contracted meningitis. Although Philipp was described as a traitor in the military newspaper, after his death the army said he died honorably (chapter 11).

Alevtina Panfilova, center, after her release from prison in May 1985. She was sentenced for two-and-one-half years in prison for helping to produce the *Prisoner Bulletin.* Galina Rytikova is on the left and Alexandra Kozorezova on the right (chapter 12).

Left: Valentina Kokurina, fifty-five, was arrested along with Alevtina Panfilova and was also sentenced for two-and-one-half years (chapter 12).

Right: Lyubov Skvortsova, twenty-four, helped Alevtina Panfilova and Valentina Kokurina with the *Prisoner Bulletin.* Lyubov was sentenced to three years in prison, which ended in early 1986 (chapter 12).

Lydiya Bondar, holding flowers,
joins with other believers in a hymn of praise
after her release from prison in April 1985 (chapter 5).

From left to right, Pastor Pavel Rytikov
(chapter 7), Vasili Ryzhuk (chapter 20), and Mikhail Petrov
hold a Bible study on a train in January 1986. Later that month on
another train, Pastor Rytikov was arrested by the KGB.

Above: On September 29, 1985, a harvest thanksgiving service in Brest is interrupted by militia and plainclothes KGB agents. The platform is warned not to proceed with the meeting (chapter 4).

Below: At the harvest thanksgiving service, the officers remove most of the roof canvas from the tent and herd the people out. They smash as much as possible and haul the canvas and other articles away in the police van (chapter 4).

9
The Ministry of Letters

Letters to believers in prison encourage them, and letters from those prisoners stir the hearts of believers in freedom to pray for them. The *Prisoner Bulletin* issued by the Council of Prisoners' Relatives regularly publishes letters from the prisoners. They not only shed light on their circumstances but reveal their spiritual comforts and the mighty keeping power of the Lord. Sometimes such letters contain nothing but praise and serve more to minister to the hearts of readers than to chronicle the writer's hardships.

Here are two examples of letters from prisoners, followed by the comments of two former prisoners about the help that they derived from letters sent to them from Christians both in the Soviet Union and overseas. The first letter is from Eduard Evert, a family man who is thirty-six years old and who comes from Makinsk. He first went to prison for the Lord in 1981 for two-and-one-half years and nine months after his release was arrested while transporting secretly printed New Testaments. He is now in prison until 1987. In prison he received a very serious hand injury while working on a lathe. This letter was sent by him to his spiritual family at the unregistered church in Makinsk.

> My warmest greetings to you, dear brothers and sisters, dear fellowship. After many months I have the opportunity and pleasure of speaking to you. I would like to take as a guiding star for both me and you, the words of Jesus in

Matthew 5:14—"A city that is set on an hill cannot be hid."
A city is the domain of living people and such a place is
always visible. Even at the darkest times, from an airplane
one sees a sea of lights. The bigger the city, the more lights
are to be seen. It is significant that Christ does not speak of
a village but of a city.

We once had a visiting preacher in Makinsk who came
from the north, and I have never forgotten one of his illus-
trations. In this man's home city the street lamps needed a
great deal of attention to keep them operational. Because of
the frequency of snow storms people lived in great danger
of getting lost, but provided they could always see the next
lamp along the road, no matter how dimly through the
snow flurries, they would find their way safely.

One day a snowstorm extinguished an entire row of
lamps along a road leading to a colliery village. Later, a man
was found frozen to death along that road. He had not wan-
dered off the track in the darkness but had died under one
of the useless lamps. He had evidently not dared to continue further because he could not see any lights. How terrible
it is for a believer to be a lamp without light. A city cannot
be hid; it is impossible when living people live in it. Even
when a fog hangs over a city, the fog itself glows like a halo.
Praise God we live in such a city! Everything in it should
shine with light—our faces, our speech, and our behavior
towards others, whether close to us or unknown to us. Such
behavior cannot remain unseen.

May God grant that no one should become lost and
freeze to death near our lamps. Christ Himself has placed
His city on the top of a hill. We are inclined to be afraid of
being highly visible, but we must not shrink from the lofty
responsibility of our Christian calling. Nothing must hide us!
I cannot hope to lose myself amongst others and disappear
out of view, but I can count on receiving from the Holy Spirit the necessary warmth and light to endure. He will create
and sustain in me the life that will shine out as heavenly
light.

When I weigh the significance of my calling, I realize
that there is something that is just as important as speaking
for Christ, and it is that Christ should be seen in me. Almost
every morning I sing to myself, as a prayer, "Jesus, my
Sun, my Joy: Thou lovest me!" This hymn has somehow

involuntarily become what is most precious to me here. "The name of the Lord is a strong tower: the righteous runneth into it, and is safe" [Proverbs 18:10]. What I am now going through is not at all similar to my first experience of imprisonment. I know of your prayers.

Your smiles in court made me indescribably joyful, and later, as I was driven from court, I saw tears on the face of a sister through the little window of the van, and I felt that I was a part of the inseparable body! How wonderfully Christ has joined us with the feelings of one body. How can you feel lonely in these circumstances? You cannot! Paul wrote, "For now we live, if ye stand fast in the Lord" [1 Thessalonians 3:8], and this is a comfort to me.

Yours with brotherly love,
Eduard Evert

Pastor Nikolai Kolbantsev, aged thirty-nine and from Rostov-on-Don, completed a two-and-one-half-year sentence in a Rostov concentration camp in 1986. He has seven children, aged four to fourteen. In this letter to his wife, Lyubov, he reflects on the question, "Am I happy here?"

Today is Sunday and I know that at this moment my friends are at the service. I have found a quiet corner for myself where there has been no noise up to now, where I cannot hear the disturbing music and where no swearing intrudes. I am writing to you as if I were holding a conversation with you. I am also turning to Him, my Friend, my Friend for life, and I know that He is with me!

There is a magnificent view from the window, a view of the seemingly endless expanse of the Steppes. I can see a canal not far away. It was empty in winter but now it is full. I can see villages in the distance, and little woods both to the right and the left.

While I look, how I wish I could just stroll out there into the endless Steppes, to walk, and walk, and walk, and never come back to this place that is so full of filth, squalor, and sin. But is everything bad here? Can I say that I am unhappy here? No, I cannot, for the Lord is with me! Even here I have enjoyed spiritual blessings.

I have spent four-and-one-half rubles in the camp shop—that is how much I had left from my monthly earnings after deductions. I bought four packets of mince, one kilo of flour sweets, and one kilo of cracknel.* You can even buy margarine in the shop, now that life has become somewhat happier and "fatter." Now that my stomach has grown accustomed to the meager diet I feel filled up by just a little fat. So don't worry—all is well. A little while ago I found it very difficult, but then I thought of the feeding of the five thousand by Christ, and I prayed—"Lord, satisfy me." After that the small amounts of food became sufficient for me, and now it is simply excellent!

One winter Sunday Ivan Leven said good-bye to his family and friends at the unregistered church of Mirolyubovka, near Omsk, and committed himself to underground service. Years of harassment by the authorities had caused this Christian to become highly noticeable in his community, and the authorities were giving indications that his arrest was imminent.

Ivan was urged by evangelical leaders, "Prison will not run away, but we need workers in the printing press. We beg you to work there for as long as it pleases the Lord." So he became a secret printer. Naturally he was not able to tell the church. As far as they were concerned he had simply "gone into the Lord's vineyard." Sacrifices were many. He could no longer visit his house, let alone his home church fellowship, for to do so would have led to his immediate arrest. Ivan felt a stunning blow of disappointment soon after his recruitment to the printing ministry when for the first time KGB officers found one of the printing units in Latvia. Then, after three years service, disaster struck Ivan's own unit. It was found by the KGB, and he was arrested in a place near Leningrad and sentenced to five years imprisonment.

Ivan has completed his sentence and has since penned the following report that shows the usefulness of sending letters to prisoners—even when they do not get through.

*One kilo equals 2.2 pounds.

Even while I was under arrest pending investigation I experienced God's wonderful guidance. It is hard being without friends and without a Bible for a long time. How greatly I longed for some comfort. But who was to give it to me? There were none but criminals around me. But nothing is impossible with God. Towards the end of my investigatory arrest I was taken to the magistrate in charge of the investigation who, in accordance with the regulations, gave me the records of the inquiries and interrogations to read through. Once I had finished with them they were to be passed back to the court. How uplifted I was to discover among the papers a card bearing the text Revelation 2:10. This had been confiscated during a house search! This text, "Be thou faithful unto death, and I will give thee a crown of life," was perfectly suited to give me great comfort at that time.

I never dared to pray for release from imprisonment because I trusted that the Lord had permitted it, and so I regarded my situation as the course desired by Him. We often ask to be His witnesses in word and deed everywhere and at all times, and in prison we can be a pointer to the living God simply by our presence. It is enough to be able to say that the Lord knows how long I am to exercise a ministry in this place.

While in prison I was never given a substantial proportion of the letters that had been sent to me. Many letters failed to arrive in the early stages of my sentence. Several times I was summoned before the prison officer responsible for the mail. Once he slammed four letters on to his desk as loudly as could be done and said, "One thing I cannot understand—this letter is from Fergana, this one from Kiev, this one from Omsk, this one from Barnaul! How come you get letters from just about everywhere?" Before I could answer he continued, "I have to admit it, you have a strong community!"

The officer in charge of my prison block once summoned me and declared, "The censors have had enough of reading letters sent to you, so they have handed all your mail over to me. I am now to examine your correspondence and decide what can be given to you. Here is a letter in German. I shall not give it to you. Who knows what is in it?" Then he handed me a beautiful postcard depicting the Last Passover with the Lord. After a moment's reflection he suddenly relented and gave me the letter in German.

> Writing letters to prisoners is definitely a good thing. It should most certainly be done faithfully. Even if the addressee does not receive everything intended for him, the fact that people are writing to him is a strong testimony to all the officials who have to read and handle these letters.

Viktor Filipishin from Khotin has recently described how important such letters were to him during his imprisonment. Viktor, now forty-seven, was released in 1984. In prison he was assigned to a manual labor section with a bad reputation, and his situation became even worse when he showed no inclination to attend political education classes, which usually include the ridiculing of God and faith.

Because of his attitude Viktor suffered the cancellation of a visit from his wife, and when he still failed to attend the classes he was placed in the punishment block. Soon the camp commandant summoned Viktor to appear before him. Viktor recalls the interview in these words.

> He held a telegram in his hand. Showing it to me he asked, "Do you know this Kozorezova?" [Mrs. Kozorezova is leader of the Council of Prisoners' Relatives.] I replied, "Yes, I know her." He then said, "I get no rest from these telegrams!"

Evidently the telegram had an effect because Viktor was then returned to the ordinary cells, and his wife was allowed her normal visiting entitlement. Some while later, Viktor was summoned before the camp commandant again. He describes the interview.

> He was holding a letter in his hand signed by numerous people. He said to me, "Listen! How much longer will this go on? Have you not had a visit?"
> "Yes," I replied, "I have had a visit."
> "Well then," he said, "how long will they keep on writing about this?"
> "They don't know I have had my visit yet. That's why they are still writing."

"Then tell them!" he commanded.

"I have already told my wife that she should tell everyone there is no longer any need for appeals concerning my visits. But we don't have radio or newspapers at our disposal to make it known to everyone instantly, and believers will continue to write until they find out," I answered.

After several days I was summoned again, and once again officers held letters in their hands. This time they were really angry with me. "Write to your wife, will you, and finally tell her to inform these people that they should not write any more. Enough is enough. You have had a visit!"

Viktor records how he was later transferred to a much stricter camp where he again had to spend time in a punishment block and forfeit his visits. This time, however, a camp officer left him in no doubt that nothing would influence them in deciding how long he would he kept in such conditions. However, in a short time he was summoned to an interview with a district attorney, who greeted him in a gentle manner and addressed him by his forename, a gesture of friendliness. Viktor's describes the conversation.

"Sit down, Viktor Yakovlevich," he said, "I intend to have a long chat with you. You know, your people have complained to the camp administration that you were unjustly placed in the punishment block, and I have been sent to clear the matter up. Why were you put in there?"

I asked him to look in my file. It said there I had refused to go to work. There was no mention of my stand on political education. After less than a week had passed a medical examination of all confinement-cell inmates was announced; an unheard of, sensational event in the camp! I sat in a cell with three other prisoners, and in a fairly short space of time it was our turn to be examined.

The doctor measured my blood pressure—it was too high. He listened to my heart and found something wrong there too. He took me along with one other very emaciated prisoner to the hospital with him. The remaining inmates of the sixteen confinement cells were not examined at all. This indicated to me that the doctor had come primarily because of numerous letters asking about the state of my health.

In the hospital I got on the scales—no one was in the room at the time—and ascertained that I had lost sixty pounds in two months. I was not put in the punishment cells again.

In a later interview with the camp commandant, he said to me, "Your wife writes, the children write, everyone writes! It is just as if you had put them up to it!" He tried to get me to stop the believers from writing, but I replied that I would continue to inform my family of the facts, though not in a complaining manner. As far as the letters from friends were concerned, I told him that I too, when free, had written on behalf of my friends, because God's love moves us to do this for each other.

On my arrival in the camp they had let me know immediately that no amount of letters would help. But I have experienced that they do help. Letters lighten the burdens of the prisoner. In such sufferings you can feel the prayers of friends. But by letters you have the evidence that your friends are devoting their time and their lives for their brother.

10

Those Counted Criminally Insane

Armed guards patrol the special psychiatric institution in Dnepropetrovsk, and they have orders to shoot to prevent any attempted escape. The complex is surrounded by a white-tiled wall surmounted by barbed wire. To ensure the protection of society there is a second wall a few yards inside the outer wall. That also is crowned with barbed wire. The buildings have iron grills over the windows. The outlook from most of them is very bleak; inmates see only other identical buildings with barred windows.

The inmates spend most of their time in their cell blocks. They are allowed into the narrow yard to walk for one hour each day. They wear black prison clothing, and their hair is closely cropped. They get little to eat and are usually maintained on high doses of powerful sedatives that slowly destroy both mind and body. The heavy staffing at Dnepropetrovsk is made up of nurses and orderlies who wear the uniforms of the staff of the ministry of the interior beneath their white coats.

No one who is sent to such a special psychiatric institution knows how long the term of confinement will be. The psychiatrists alone will determine whether the inmate continues to represent a danger to himself and to others, and the final word lies with the courts. Many years may pass before the inmate emerges from such an institution. To be released he must make two definite affirmations: first, that he realizes he was ill at the time he committed his criminal deed, and second, that he was wrong to do what he did.

The offenders in such special psychiatric institutions have usually committed murder or rape, but there are also people who have committed the offense of giving their children a religious upbringing, or of convening prayer meetings, or of having led a Christian young people's choir. At the time of writing, six believers from unregistered Baptist churches are known to be in special psychiatric institutions—five men and one woman.

Anna Vasilievna Chertkova has been in a psychiatric unit in Tashkent for fourteen years. One can only imagine what this woman, now fifty-eight years old, has gone through all this time. Anna's elderly mother wrote the following to the minister of the interior of the USSR: "Our daughter Anna Vasilievna Chertkova only professed her faith in God, and this led to a prison sentence. In 1972 she was committed to a psychiatric institution where she is to this day. She is of sound mind, but will not be released because she will not renounce her faith in God."

At the Tashkent institution, patients exercise in an area measuring two yards wide by thirty yards long. A patient will not see or touch a blade of grass anywhere. Anna is regularly injected with the strongest tranquilizers, and while her physical health is fair, her mental condition is gradually declining.

Eight years ago, believer Anatoli Fyodorovich Runov (then forty-one years old) was arrested and committed to a Leningrad psychiatric institution. The official diagnosis of his condition was schizophrenia, but Mrs. Runova testifies that Anatoli had been harassed by the KGB for the previous twelve years because of his Christian activities.

She appealed to the general prosecutor of the USSR in these words: "Being completely healthy and sane, my husband is now isolated behind the prison walls of a psychiatric hospital." Four years ago he was offered his freedom on condition that he give up preaching. Anatoli gave the following reply: "Prisons, exile, and institutions serve as pulpits for the people of Jesus."

He was released soon after that but not for long. Within six months he was arrested again and taken to the special psychiatric unit at Gorki, from which he has not been released. Anatoli has had his Bible confiscated on the grounds that he is too sick to be allowed to read it. His medication has led to severe side effects, including very high blood pressure, tremors in arms and legs, and amnesia.

Arkadi Pavlovich Ivanov, aged fifty-four and father of ten, has been held in a special psychiatric institution at Kazan since September 1983 after having been declared of unsound mind by a court. In the following year he was allowed only one visit, lasting half an hour, from his wife. A doctor at the institution told him that he would be allowed to go home if he succeeded in persuading his wife and children to renounce God. In June of last year Arkadi was moved to a psychiatric institution in Yoshkar-Ola.

Viktor Semyenovich Bessubenko, from Zhdanov, and Vyacheslav Viktorovich Minkov are both young men who were committed to psychiatric institutions when they were called up for national service some two years ago and sought to witness for the Lord. Vyacheslav Minkov was sent to a psychiatric institution at Chernigov, where relatives were told that he would be classified as schizophrenic for as long as he continued to speak about God.

Vladimir Pavlovich Khailo, from Voroshilovgrad, Ukraine, has been in the special psychiatric institution in Dnepropetrovsk since 1980, when he was declared to be of unsound mind by a court and sent for compulsory psychiatric treatment. On arrival at the institution Vladimir was put in a room crowded with twenty-seven other people. They literally had to climb over each other to get into bed. A month after his admission, Mariya Khailo was allowed to visit her husband. She reported: "When I arrived there I could scarcely recognize him. His skin had become very dark because of the drugs he was given."

Since then, Vladimir Khailo's health has so deteriorated

that he suffers chest pains, his hands will not function, and he cannot raise his right arm.

Vladimir later sustained a reaction to drugs that caused his entire body to become swollen. His sight grew suddenly worse, and he lost consciousness. He was then given an injection that gave rise to very painful symptoms such as aching limbs and high fever. At one stage a doctor told him, "Admit that you are ill and renounce all that you have done and even today you could go free. Alternatively we must continue to feed you up with tablets."

On another occasion a woman doctor sent for Vladimir and said very directly to him, "You are not suffering from schizophrenia but from a neurosis. You have divided thoughts. If you are agreeable we will put you before a commission that can release you so that you can go back to work. You must simply agree to attend only the services of a registered church and to preach only there." Vladimir answered, "I cannot give you my agreement because I serve the Lord and not man."

Mariya Khailo sought to have the actions of the staff investigated by petitioning her local office of justice, but she was warned that if she pressed her petition she would only make things worse for her husband. Although protest has so far proved unavailing in the case of Vladimir Khailo, there are many instances where publicity and appeals both in the USSR and the West have had a helpful effect. The Soviet authorities dislike these acts of cruelty being spoken of throughout the world.

Vladimir Khailo is now fifty-four. One of his letters home to his large family characterizes his attitude toward his trials. He makes no complaints but chiefly counsels his family to view his imprisonment as a spiritual trial.

> I have committed you into Christ's hands, my children. He invites us to come to Him to learn meekness and humility from Him and to find peace not only for the body but above all for the soul. The body is passing, but the soul is eternal.

Therefore, dear children, I do not ask you if you have enough to eat and wear. I know that Christ cares for you day and night. If in His mercy He feeds the birds, will He then forsake you? Can He forsake His declaration that He is the Father of the orphans? Let us therefore be filled with love and compassion for our persecutors. Revenge and cursing should flee from us. Instead we should want to pray for them. They would not hold me here another day longer, if there were no orders from above. For me, this means that the Lord allows it! Dear children, be obedient to your mother, and ease her burdens. She has done so much for you —make her happy by your obedience. Be patient and be at peace with one another, and also be at peace in your hearts.

Mariya Khailo appealed in a letter published in the *Prisoner Bulletin:* "Dear loved ones of the Lord, I appeal to you with this great need: Cry out to God in prayer for my family and for my husband who has been forcibly interned in a psychiatric hospital!"

Up till now, the chief physician at Dnepropetrovsk, Dr. Anatoli Semiryazhko, and his deputy, Dr. Alexander Khabarov, have only indicated that this "patient" must continue to be detained indefinitely unless he is cured of his religious views.

11

Cruelties to Young Servicemen

Young Baptists serving in the Soviet army are constantly subjected to persecution for their religious convictions. Often that persecution is extremely cruel. When these young men are first registered for military service the word "Baptist" is printed in large red letters on their documents. From that moment, such men are recorded in a special file at the ministry of defense of the USSR, indicating that they need compulsory reeducation. This reeducation is accomplished by such methods as beatings, torture, or imprisonment, and in certain instances it has resulted in death. All those activities are conducted by the military section of the KGB.

The persecution of Christian conscripts is nothing new. The case of Ivan Moiseyev has been given extensive publicity around the world. In 1972 this young man serving in a Soviet army unit in the Crimea was subjected to brutal torture for his faith in Christ and then drowned in the Azov Sea near the city of Kerch. In 1977 Nikolai Kravchenko, then serving in a Soviet military unit in the city of Kursk, was beaten up by two officers of his unit. The result of his "ideological reeducation" was a double fracture of the lower jaw, resulting in severe pinching of the facial nerves. Nikolai became disabled and in need of a serious operation, but the Soviet authorities would not give any medical aid or pension support.

When a young conscript's church fellowship hears about such beatings, they often write to the government or to the military unit to plead for understanding, and surprisingly they

sometimes receive replies. Here is a reply from the commander of a military unit that sets out this officer's reasons young
believers must be treated harshly on account of their religious
views and activities.

(1) Any religious belief must be pure imagination, because
there are countless different opinions about beliefs and
every believer considers his faith the only right one.

(2) The authorities do not close their eyes to injustices. On
the contrary they expose them. There is one law for
all—the constitution of the USSR—and the minority is
subject to the majority. Therefore we advise you to give
up your religious convictions and to think about your
duty in the present life.

(3) According to statistics the community of believers is
made up of pensioners and women, of whom 42 percent are illiterate. Nor is that surprising, otherwise they
would know of the resolutions of the ninth and tenth
Congresses of Evangelical Christians, which recognized
military service.* Your faith can only be explained by
your inexcusable backwardness, which resembles the
condition of stone-age man.

(4) Although you frighten yourselves and others with the
notion of a life after death and God's judgment, it appears that after all you do value this earthly life, and
you see very clearly that it is better to be in freedom
than in prison. This is why you had the audacity to
write to the defense minister himself and threaten him
with God's judgment to let you go free now.

Therefore, keep the written earthly laws and not the
ones invented by yourselves out of idleness and illiter-
acy.

Vladimir Tarazovich Sokogon,
Commander of Military Unit 63324, Kirovabad

A few years ago two eighteen-year-old believers, Vladimir Muzyka and Philipp Korniyenko, received their call-up pa-

---

*These congresses, organized by the registered Baptists and manipulated
by the authorities, pass resolutions that may be used against young believers who refuse to take the communist oath.

pers and went to serve in the Soviet armed services. Only a few months later their dead bodies were brought home. What happened to these young men, both sons of pastors of unregistered churches in the Cherkassy region of the Ukraine?

In the USSR, the place to which an enlisted serviceman will be posted is kept strictly secret. He is simply ordered to report to military headquarters; from there groups of conscripts are collected by officers and noncommissioned officers of the units where they will be trained. These officers never say where they have come from. The young men are taken into an unknown future.

Vladimir Muzyka, from Uman, had been thinking about military service for a long time and felt unable, as a matter of conscience, to take the military oath. He made known his decision not to take the oath at his first interview at the Uman military headquarters. "You will never come home alive!" the commander said to him.

When Vladimir left home his parents waited to see which part of the USSR their son would write from. After nearly four weeks the long-desired letter came. Vladimir was stationed at Semipalatinsk in eastern Kazakhstan. He wrote that he had been to interviews twice about his refusal to take the oath, but the second time the authorities had begun to intimidate him. His parents knew that Vladimir was sparing them the brutal truth about what had happened to him.

Nothing further was heard until one month later, when a telegram arrived with the terse message, "Your son Vladimir has died suddenly. Please indicate your wishes for his burial by telegram." The telegram came from a unit in Lessosibirsk, to which Vladimir had evidently been moved.

The stunned parents elected to have his funeral in their hometown, and within a week a military delegation arrived in Uman with their son's body. Strangely, they had no death certificate or other documentation to indicate how he had died. Only when the parents repeatedly and insistently asked for information did the local military commander seek an explanation from the unit at Lessosibirsk.

A telegram reply stated that the cause of death was suppuration of the brain. A postmortem had found two large pus-filled abscesses in the young man's brain, one 3.5 x 3 centimeters and the other 5 x 5 centimeters.* The most likely cause of such a condition—severe head injuries—was not mentioned in the telegram.

When Vladimir's parents visited the Lessosibirsk unit they found that he had complained of severe head pains on arrival from Semipalatinsk. He had reported to the medical room where he was given some simple medication. When roused the next morning he had not managed to get dressed and order his kit in the time allowed and had been reprimanded accordingly. As the days progressed he had become so weak that he could not even button up his quilted jacket, and a sergeant had detailed another soldier to help him. Nevertheless, he had still been sent on training duties in outside temperatures below -40°C (-40°F).

A fellow conscript gave an account of Vladimir's last day. At four o'clock in the morning he got out of bed and fell suddenly to the ground. Other men carried him to the medical room but were not allowed to wait with him. At nine o'clock one of them went back to the medical room, but Vladimir lay dead, covered with a sheet.

*   *   *

The Korniyenko family received the telegram that told of the death of their son, Philipp, three months after his enlistment. It read: "Your son Philipp has died in the course of duty. Come immediately. Confirm your response by telegram. Utin, Unit Commander."

On arrival at his unit the parents were told that their son

*1.37 x 1.18 inches and 2 x 2 inches.

had contracted meningitis that had developed so rapidly that he was dead within two days. The cause of death was described in the death certificate as "Inflammation of the brain applying pressure to the cerebellum in the foramen magnum."

The Korniyenkos wrote to the defense ministry saying that they could accept his death if they could be certain that he had died from an unavoidable condition, following normal treatment. However, they had discovered that Philipp had been constantly terrorized for refusing the military oath. He had been slandered before the whole regiment, threatened with legal proceedings, and held in the guardroom. What had happened to him while there? A special officer had been sent from a unit five hundred miles away to bring pressure on him to change his mind, and he had been described as a traitor in a military newspaper.

Strangely, immediately after his death the army had revised its opinion of him and decided to classify him as one who had died "honorably" in the course of his duties. The authorities had not allowed the parents to bury their son quietly according to the custom of believers. A contingent of officers and men, together with a few dozen unknown men in civilian clothes who were treated with great respect by the uniformed men, had been assigned to attend the funeral, and district officials also showed extraordinary interest in the event.

The parents naturally speculated on what had moved such people—who were normally so hostile to the Korniyenko family—to bestow all this honor on their son in public. Were they trying to demonstrate that the authorities were innocent of the death of a Christian?

* * *

Sergei Petrenko was serving in a unit at Leninsk when he was dragged out of bed at night and taken to a room for interrogation. A sergeant entered and punched him in the face twice. The sergeant ordered Sergei to kneel before him, and when he refused he was hit and kicked. The next morning he was unrecognizable. His right cheek was gashed and his face so swollen that it was impossible for him to eat. Such treatment was maintained for three months, and when he complained to a superior officer he was beaten even more brutally.

Sergei wrote home saying,

> I would like to share my trials . . . actually I am already getting used to them, but it is unpleasant for the body as well as the soul. Not one day passes without someone hitting me, but just recently I have been badly beaten up, to say nothing of minor abuses like punches in the face or kicks. They were all so drunk that they did not care where or how hard they hit me. Afterwards I could only just stand up and my back was as stiff as a plank. . . . They tried to get me to kneel before the sergeant-major and worship him. He said, "I am God, worship me!" They beat me and then gave me the most arduous possible work to do. . . . For my part I try to meet them with love.

Sergei's parents made strenuous complaints, and his treatment improved. The unit commander wrote: "The facts you and your son report have been confirmed in part. The offenders, Sergeant Tamkus and Sergeant Belyakov, have been subject to disciplinary proceedings and have been censured and demoted. They have apologized to your son. However, no 'cruel tortures' as you allege took place."

*   *   *

At the time of writing, a young man named Yuri Burda is the last known conscript to have lost his life in highly suspicious circumstances. A young Baptist from the village of Posharskoya in the Crimea, Yuri declined to take the military oath at the beginning of his national service. A major ominously retorted, "Then we will work on you!" He was posted to a unit at Semipalatinsk, but within a few months his parents received the telegram that told them that their son had tragically lost his life.

Yuri's parents, accompanied by their eldest son, took the long air journey to Semipalatinsk. On arrival they were met by Major Pavlov, the unit's officer responsible for political education, and also by the local magistrate appointed to investigate the death. Yuri's father recorded what took place.

> I immediately asked, "Did Yuri die in a motor accident?" Major Pavlov answered, "No." He then explained that the cause of death was an accident in which Yuri had been electrocuted. After finishing work he had parked his vehicle and gone to a wash basin [presumably a metal one] by the garage. He took off his shoes and began to wash his feet with cold water. At that moment the electric light hanging over the sink short circuited. Yuri lost his balance, grabbed the basin with both hands, and emitted a loud groan. A man standing nearby named Igor Bereshnoi pulled him away from the sink.

Mr. Burda was not satisfied with the major's story, and he pressed for further information. "How was it that Yuri died," he asked, "while the other man suffered no harm? How long was my son under the current?" When Mr. Burda asked to see the scene of the accident, Major Pavlov insisted that this was impossible because the unit was in a restricted area. The parents would be able to hear all the details from those who witnessed the tragedy. Mr. Burda asked the major if he knew that Yuri was a believer and whether he had taken the military oath. "Yes, we knew," replied Major Pavlov, "and he did not take the oath. But we did not put him under any pressure because of that."

After this conversation the examining magistrate began to ask the Burdas many questions that only increased their alarm and suspicions about Yuri's death. For three hours he quizzed them about Yuri's upbringing: his religious activities, his friends, whether or not his religious sect was opposed to national service, and whether he had written home about the behavior of his superior officers to him. With the day almost over, Yuri's body had still not been produced, nor had the promised witnesses of the tragedy. The Burdas went to a local hotel.

The following morning, when the coffin was due to be handed over in time for an early flight, the unit commander arrived to say that it would not be ready for another eight hours. However, when the time arrived, there was still no sign of the coffin—or the witnesses—and the Burdas had to fly home without it.

When the coffin eventually arrived, it was opened in the presence of a large gathering of relatives and villagers. Mr. Burda's account makes harrowing reading.

> Yuri's body had been dissected. His hands were by no means clean; his tongue together with its tendons had been torn out. His eyes looked as though they were coated with a grey film, his hands were disjointed and could be freely moved in all directions, and blue marks encircled his wrists, indicative of handcuffs.
>
> His fingers were completely crushed flat, and black in color. His arms were covered in pin pricks up to the elbow, and on his upper arms and shoulders were four punctures with burn marks, like the marks from electrical contacts. There were similar punctures on his temples and chin. Yuri's heart had also been punctured and the edges of this wound showed the same scorch marks. The body had been drained of blood. Yuri's hair was gray.

The Burda family has still not received a death certificate, and all that they have seen and heard convinces them that Yuri died as the result of violent intimidation.

*   *   *

Two servicemen are known to have been committed to psychiatric institutions solely because of their religious convictions. Vyacheslav Minkov, from Minsk, was placed under com-

pulsory psychiatric treatment in April 1984. When called up to
the forces he refused to take the military oath on grounds of
conscience. Three times he was transferred to different units
where he was pressed to take the oath. In his final posting his
fellow trainees were encouraged to beat him up several times,
viciously kicking him in the face with their boots. At temperatures of -40°C (-40°F) he was repeatedly thrown out of the
barracks on to the streets for the night. The violent intimidation continued for about three months until he was sent to a
psychiatric hospital in the town of Chernigov in the Ukraine.
When his sister visited him she was told, "As long as he talks
about God, we will consider him schizophrenic."

Another young believer named Viktor Semyenovich Bessubenko was also put in a psychiatric institution when he
made it clear that he was a believer.

The believers from the unregistered Baptist churches do
not complain about the general level of rough treatment that
is faced by all conscripts to the Soviet armed services. Nor do
they protest at what they call the "more normal" blows and
kicks, which believing servicemen take for granted. Many
young Christians have to endure such torments during their
national service. However, for some, the level of violence
reaches terrible proportions. A number of young believers
have been beaten so much that severe concussion of the brain
has led to their being dismissed from the army as invalids.
Such deaths occurring in horrific circumstances must lead to
widely publicized protest on the part of believers.

It should be mentioned that many believers complete
their service fairly normally, suffering little more than all the
other soldiers. There are many unit commanders who have
believing parents, and such officers are quite well-disposed
towards believers. Other officers are expecting promotion,
and that comes most surely to those who have "peaceful"
units. In those cases a commander will often turn a blind eye
when a young man refuses to take the oath on grounds of
conscience.

In general, however, national service brings the believer

to a time of great testing, and the young men who are called to face this unpredictable, often brutal, and sometimes even fatal event in their lives should be supported by the prayer of believers everywhere.

12

The Women Prisoners

"There are sometimes such difficult moments that you just long to be able to leap over the fence and disappear. But then your soul finds peace, and you say to the Lord: I do not ask for release, but preserve me, protect me, and help me to remain faithful and to withstand everything without murmuring."

These words were written by Valentina Kokurina, aged fifty-five, in a letter from a camp in Odessa where she served a two-and-one-half-year prison sentence along with Alevtina Panfilova, who is forty-nine. These two women lived together in Voroshilovgrad, where they put their house at the disposal of the Council of Prisoners' Relatives. To help the work of the council ranks as a serious crime carrying heavy penalties, yet many women, like Valentina and Alevtina, are prepared to risk all to help in the Lord's work.

One day in February 1983, KGB officers burst into their house and found typewriters and papers that demonstrated that they were workers in the production of the *Prisoner Bulletin*. Both were later sentenced to two-and-one-half years of imprisonment and sent to a women's camp in Odessa.

How would two middle-aged women survive the rigors of such a sentence? Even young, healthy people invariably return from these centers of misery utterly emaciated and sick. During the first year of their sentences they both suffered severe deterioration of health. In addition, heartless cruelties were inflicted on them when the camp authorities disallowed all visits to them on the grounds that those visiting were not immediate relatives. (The two women had no immediate relatives.)

In her letters Valentina revealed that she suffered from frequent attacks of fainting and from painful eyes. When she finished her daily work she had to go straight to bed to recover her strength for the next shift. She did not complain, however, but wrote, ''I try to speak to my heavenly Father above about my pains. He supports me and helps me.''

In a concentration camp it is not easy to find a quiet place where you can pray. Everywhere there are always prisoners. Some quarrel, while others mock, swear, and shout. Prisoners have to work long and hard. So believers must wait until nightfall before they can pour out their distress before the Lord. Only by prayer can they endure life in a concentration camp.

How else could they bear with patience the crushing disappointments that are inflicted on them? Expected letters are often not handed over. Visits are canceled. Money that is earned from prison work, vital for buying little essentials in the camp shop, is suddenly reduced by half. In one letter Valentina Kokurina wrote: ''Alya [the familiar name of Alevtin] was promised a long-term visit on January 25, and yesterday it was suddenly canceled.''

Valentina was unable to meet the work quotas because she could scarcely move her hands and feet. In spite of this she was forced to continue working. She wrote:

> Through God's grace I am kept every day and strengthened. I do not give up, although my health makes me vulnerable. But, the Lord be praised, He comes to me so quickly with His love and help and gives me courage to hope in Him. He never disappoints my trust, and His living Word, which dwells in my heart, is a light on my way. As David said—''I rejoice at thy word, as one that findeth great spoil.''
>
> The final year of my sentence has begun. Although it is a long time, He will not leave me. In the coming year I will turn fifty-five—retiring age. The years have flown like a

dream. Yet what is our life? A vapor that can be seen for a brief while and then disappears. And then comes our meeting with the Lord. May He help us always to be ready for our happy meeting with Him.

Alevtina suffered especially during her sentence because her heart was weak. She wrote this while in prison:

During the night of the twenty-ninth my heart was so bad that at morning roll call at 5:30 A.M. I scarcely had the strength to wash, dress, and prepare for work. I made my bed and went slowly to the brigade leader, told her I did not have the strength to go to work, and wished to report to the doctor.

At first the brigade leader would not accept it and ordered me to go to work. I tried obediently but my hands would not obey. As time went by I sat weeping and prayed for help. Then the brigade leader came up to me and ordered me to lie down for a while and then to report to the doctor. So I stayed in bed until nine o'clock and then dragged myself slowly to the doctor, who was a woman.

She examined me, but murmured for a while saying that given the same state of health at home I would have cared for myself, lit the oven, cooked my meals, and so on. I replied that in such a state I would have to lie down at home also. The doctor took my blood pressure but did not tell me the result. She told me that I was in exactly the same condition as a month earlier when I was brought to her by ambulance from the work area.

I thought to myself that if she did not certify me sick I would have to go to the barracks to lie down, even if they put me in the punishment block for it. I would rather die of cold there on the concrete floor. She muttered at me again for a long time. I said, "Well, do I have to go back?" "No," she replied, and signed me sick for three days.

And now I have been lying here for three days and can neither eat nor drink, though I am a little better. But what can I do? Can I go to her again? I would rather collapse. They can carry me wherever they want to then! The doctor has obviously been ordered not to release me from work. How can I think otherwise when I do not have the strength to stand up and even need support to sit up because I am so weak? Yet we are thankful for everything. Another day has passed—thanks be to the Lord for that!

It is winter now and the washing does not dry properly. It hangs in the barracks. Every night is the same—dampness, a lack of fresh air, and you cannot breathe. That is why the nights are so painful. And so it goes on today, tomorrow, and the day after tomorrow.

Obviously, imprisoned believers do not tell the worst of their problems to their relatives because it would be too upsetting. But their letters contain enough to spur us on to prayer and to show how the Lord gives His children strength to keep their Christian bearing even in difficult circumstances. Alevtina once wrote: "We do not despair. We are thankful for everything and wait for His impending return to us. We long to go to heaven—to go home."

Lyubov Skvortsova, whose home is in Gagra, was working on the *Prisoner Bulletin* at the house of Valentina and Alevtina at the time of the KGB search, and she also was arrested. She was twenty-four at the time and was given a three-year sentence, which ended early in 1986. Lyubov was sent to a women's concentration camp at Kharkov, where within a year she became very ill, and her hair began to fall out. In 1985 she wrote the following sentiments in a letter addressed to "all her friends at home and abroad."

> Everything is very much alive and precious in my memory. We are all one family in the Lord, and our joys and sorrows are shared joys and sorrows. We have the same outlook on life, and the same heavenly Father. I am now in much better health, but I worry about you. You are having a difficult time at the moment. . . . The certain way to help one another is to pray for one another. Prayer accomplishes many things! What great power it has!
>
> I could never have stood alone in this battle, but through your prayers the Lord has given me strength and health. Things are not so difficult for me now. We receive warm, kind letters from friends, and thus we live with God's

help. A heartfelt greeting to all friends. Also a very, very heartfelt greeting to friends abroad. A parcel was sent to me from Belgium. Naturally it was not given to me, but it was forwarded to my mother. Thank you to you all.

Other women prisoners have been convicted for teaching children in Sunday schools or for being involved with the work of the secret printing presses or the distribution of literature. Alexandra Kozorezova, leader of the Council of Prisoners' Relatives, wrote a report on the conditions of women prisoners in which she said that their environment and treatment was no better than that of men prisoners. She gave details of the following prisoners:

> Valentina Saveleva, aged thirty-one, and Evelina Zhukovskaya, aged forty-five, have the longest sentences to serve —each having five years. What were their crimes to merit such severe sentences? Valentina was arrested in January 1982 and found to be in possession of Christian literature for children. After being sentenced she was forced to work in a concentration camp for twelve to fourteen hours a day. Through this she became utterly exhausted. Many prayers and appeals have led to her working time being recently reduced to normal levels.
>
> Evelina was arrested in May 1983 after a house search that revealed Christian literature and cassettes. Before their arrests both women lived near Stavropol to the north of the Caucasus. Not far away, in the town of Mozdok, three other Christian women were arrested and imprisoned in August 1983— Natalya Chervyakova (then thirty-one) and her cousins, the Shvetsova sisters Anna (twenty-one) and Dina (twenty-two). The background to their arrest was that part of the church in Mozdok gave in to official pressure demanding that the church become registered. However, two-thirds of the fellowship, including the young people, did not accept that compromise with the authorities. Thus Natalya, who led the choir, and the Shvetsova sisters, who organized the Sunday school, were arrested.

In recent years the number of women from the unregistered Baptist churches who are held in prisons or psychiatric institutions has never fallen below ten, and at times has reached twenty-five. That figure does not include short sentences of less than a year. The average sentence is three years. To Western readers, the best known woman prisoner is probably Galina Vilchinskaya, who, at the time of writing, is at home after completing her second prison term. Galina's experiences are recounted in chapter 3. The longest serving prisoner is Anna Chertkova, aged fifty-eight, who has been in a Tashkent psychiatric institution for over thirteen years.

This review of some of the women sufferers barely scratches the surface of what has been endured over the last twenty-five years by so many active believers within the unregistered fold. Numerous young women have forfeited their youth and health in labor camps in the far north, while an equally large number of older women, including grandmothers, have been stripped of all comfort and dignity to suffer in a way that would not be inflicted upon the worst criminal in the West.

13

My Path to Prison

Pastor Nikolai Baturin is a pastor of the fellowship meeting at Shakhty, near Rostov, and is also a member of the Council of Unregistered Baptist Churches. He has been persecuted for thirty-eight years. He was first imprisoned when only twenty and has now served twenty years in prison plus terms of exile in the far north. He was last arrested in November 1979 while he was underground and was sentenced to five years imprisonment.

In September 1983, he was suddenly transferred to a prison for those awaiting trial on new charges. That resulted in a further two-year sentence to be added to his present term. (His release date is now November 1986.) Here is Pastor Baturin's own account of his life and trials.

Pastor Baturin's Story

I was born on December 15, 1927, in Ilanski, near Kanski in the northeast of Russia. My father had come to know Christ in 1920, and persecution soon followed. In the year that I was born he was elected pastor of his congregation, the previous pastor having been imprisoned. Just two years later, new laws led to a great increase of persecution for Christians. My father was relieved of his right to vote because he was a pastor and had special taxes imposed upon him. He also suffered several terms of imprisonment lasting between two and three months each. Other hardships were then devised for him.

My grandfather owned an eighty-acre small holding on which we grew vegetables, and he gave my father a one-third share in the land. In 1932 the authorities ordered my father to produce an impossible quantity of two-and-one-half tons of vegetables as tax due the state, but he could only achieve about half of that amount. The state took the entire yield, together with our only cow, leaving nothing for the family to live on.

Soon afterwards the state exiled my father to the far north for five years, although he was allowed to come home before the time was up. However, his freedom was short-lived, for in 1936 he was arrested along with all the other preachers of the region of Krasnoyarsk. We only saw him once after that. I was a schoolboy at the time and still remember the day when we were allowed to visit him in prison. Only years afterwards did we learn that he had died of anemia in a concentration camp in 1941.

There were four children in our family, and our mother went out to work to support us. Obviously, she was not able to pamper us. As far as our Baptist church in Krasnoyarsk was concerned, the meetings came to an end because all the preachers were arrested. As far as I remember, between thirty and forty brethren were imprisoned. When the meetings ceased, my mother started to read the New Testament to us and sing hymns every evening.

I was not a good boy and at the age of thirteen caused my mother a great deal of worry. But then I felt a desire in my heart to change my ways and began to seek to live as a Christian. I withdrew from the general pursuits that I had been involved in with other youngsters and began to pray and to read the Word of God.

At fourteen I joined in the services that resumed in my hometown and began to study at the Technical Engineer's School for the Construction of Steam Locomotives in Krasnoyarsk. Soon afterwards I came to a personal knowledge of the Lord, and in October 1945, at the age of seventeen, I was among forty young people baptized at our church. It was the first baptism since the mid-thirties. In the next four years many young people came into the church, a large number of them students.

Once I had left the engineering school in 1947, I became very involved in the young people's work of my church, which by this time had been officially registered. It is now well-known that registration was designed to restrict the activities of the churches. Our efforts were greatly concentrated in evangelism, and so we attracted the attention of the security forces. They were determined to stop the flow of young people streaming into our fellowship.

First the pastor was arrested. Then, a few months later (on August 27, 1948), three active younger people, including myself, were arrested. I was then twenty years of age and was engaged to be married to a Christian girl named Valentina. After six months detention pending investigation, I was sentenced to ten years imprisonment without trial by the Select Committee of the Ministry for State Security.

The summary of evidence against me read:

> The accused has not sung any Soviet songs; has not read any Soviet literature; has not been to any Soviet clubs, theatres or cinemas, but on the contrary he has attended the meetings of the Baptist sectarians, has sung religious songs, idolized life after death, and given religious sermons. He has thereby turned away from sociopolitical life himself and has incited others to do the same.

I was sent to a concentration camp at Vorkuta, a town inside the Arctic Circle; but after exactly seven years, I was released, on condition that I did not leave Vorkuta. Valentina, with whom I had corresponded through those years, had agreed to share my earthly pathway of suffering, and she came up to Vorkuta where we were married. After our first child was born, we were granted permission to leave the region.

We moved to Shakhty in the Rostov area in the Ukraine and joined a registered church there. The young people and a few of the older brethren received us with great joy, but the pastor acted very coldly towards us. We soon discovered why. This pastor had been intimidated into forbidding any meetings, especially the youth meetings, which would encourage church growth. The pastor had frequently threatened the young people that they would have to be reported and imprisoned if they held meetings in their homes against the rules.

Shortly after our arrival in Shakhty my wife and I were invited to a prohibited meeting. It was a meeting full of blessing. We had scarcely left the house when the pastor arrived —too late—to prevent the meeting taking place. Since I had been imprisoned already, it was clear that my presence would not please a pastor who had already allowed the local controller of religious affairs to manipulate him.

The more evangelistic members of the church, especially the young people, pressed the pastor to appoint me to the preaching ministry, and thus he reluctantly allowed me into the pulpit from time to time. A prayer circle was formed in the church, and also a Bible study circle—groups that were to play a vital role in difficulties that we were about to encounter.

Early in 1959 a secret government directive was issued that ordered the closure, under any suitable pretext, of all meeting places of registered evangelical Christian Baptists. Some convenient infringement of the laws governing religious services or any technical defect in the building would serve as a pretext. In the case of our church, a visiting commission soon found that our building was in need of repair and that the toilets were located too close to the meeting area. The church was duly closed.

At first we attended neighboring churches, but at the beginning of 1960 those of us in our prayer and Bible study group—there were twelve of us—began to seek guidance as to whether we should hold our own meetings in our homes. The pastor and elders of our fellowship attacked us vehemently for this. They declared that they had hoped to obtain permission to repair the church building and accused us of obstructing a successful outcome through our conduct.

In the course of the year, half of the churches in the Rostov area were closed, including the church in the very center of the town, and we later heard that the authorities had received special privileges for their achievements in the fight against religion. As a result of those things, twelve of us became firmly convinced that the Lord wanted us to hold services in our homes. The plan spread quickly among the believers in the town so that more and more people came to meet with us. Yet only one deacon from the dissolved registered churches came. The others kept well away and attended no meetings of any kind.

When an action group arose among evangelical Baptists in 1961, we supported the proposal for a conference wholeheartedly. A year later our church, which had grown quite large, elected me along with two other brethren to serve as pastors. I was also appointed to take part in the organizing committee for the action group conference. This work, together with preaching and pastoral ministry, required that I give up my job. I had been in full-time Christian service for six weeks when I was arrested for living a parasitic life, and, being found guilty of "sponging," I was exiled to the Irkutsk area for five years.

Believers from many churches were exiled at that time, but such measures could not retard the spiritual life that was bursting forth in many awakened churches. During my exile a printed magazine representing our point of view—*Herald of Salvation*—was first produced. A copy was passed to me by another believer and I read it through with great joy before passing it on.

Shortly afterwards the KGB searched our home and interrogated me about the magazine. They wanted to know who the publishers were, whether I was involved in it, and where the magazine was produced. The authorities were clearly extremely agitated because such a magazine was bound to have great influence.

In 1965, believers experienced a respite from persecution largely as the result of the martyrdom of Nikolai Khmara in the prison at Barnaul in the previous year. The evangelical Baptist congregations at Barnaul and Kulunda, where the Khmara family lived, appealed to the government with the support of believers throughout the land. Many letters were sent to the government demanding that the murder of imprisoned believers be stopped.

After Mr. Khrushchev was overthrown in October 1964, many believers obtained early release from imprisonment and exile, and I was among them. It was in March 1965 that I was able to return to my home church at Shakhty. However, the ebb tide did not last for long, and a new wave of persecution was soon launched. Evangelical Baptists decided to submit their problems to the new leader of the government, Mr. Brezhnev. On May 16, 1966, several hundred believers went to Moscow to ask for an audience, but they were all arrested the next day. I was among them. Like many of the other delegates sent from the churches, I was sentenced to three years imprisonment.

I served my sentence in a concentration camp near Rostov and was glad that I could stay near my hometown. However, it soon became obvious that this was no gesture of friendliness from the authorities, for I was subjected to the close attention of the KGB. The visits from KGB officers began about a year before the end of my sentence. They chatted with me, took a sympathetic interest in my health, inquired into the well-being of my family, and so on. They made great efforts to reduce the alienation and suspicion that I obviously felt concerning them and tried to make me feel accustomed to their presence.

Looking back, I would say that those officers were well selected and trained for their role. They could talk about anything. Slowly and almost unnoticeably, they could bring a conversation round to what they wanted to talk about—the life of my church. In such conversations the questions were asked so skillfully that until one gained experience, one could give away some fragment of valuable information without realizing one had done so. Many things were of interest to the KGB. Among other things they wanted to know who the leader of the church was, who the active members were, who performed the baptisms, and who had recently been baptized.

Two areas of activity particularly disturbed the KGB. Those were the work of the Council of Prisoners' Relatives and the work of the secret Christian publishing house. When those were the subject of conversation I would always repeat what all prisoners say—that the authorities have themselves created these organizations. I would tell them that if they only stopped persecuting believers and released the prisoners, the existence of the Council of Prisoners' Relatives would become unnecessary.

As far as the publishing house was concerned, I would tell them that our Council of Unregistered Churches had submitted a request to the government to be permitted to print ten thousand Bibles as well as hymnbooks and a religious magazine. That written request had been ignored. I would tell the officers that there was a very great need for spiritual literature in our churches, and therefore we were forced to make some provision. As soon as we received official permission to print our literature, the secret work would become superfluous.

When my sentence was over, I became fully involved again in the work of our brotherhood and sought to fulfill my duties with all the energy I possessed. Then, three years later, I was rearrested and sentenced to four years imprisonment. My sentence began in March 1973, but this time I was sent to Komi, ASSR*—a northern European part of Russia.

At first I was placed in a joinery factory and put to work

*Armenian Soviet Socialist Republic.

with a planing machine. However, following a visit from a Rostov KGB official my situation changed. He told me that the All-Union Council of Evangelical Christian Baptist Churches (the governing body of registered Baptist churches) had received permission to hold a national conference, and he asked me if I would like to take part.

I was amazed that a prisoner should be asked such a question, for I had never yet heard of prisoners being given leave to travel as delegates to conferences. However, the official explained to me that captivity was a relative concept! By the very next day I would be free if I would only go to the conference and contribute along the lines that he would give me. The officer even promised that I would subsequently be allowed to carry on my ministry in my church, be with my family, and would not need to work for my living in the factory. The only condition would be that every now and then I would have to meet with some of his colleagues to discuss some details of our church's activity. In other words, the condition was full cooperation with the KGB.

It was obvious that I had been approached because I was a member of the Council of Unregistered Churches. They wanted me to participate in a conference of registered churches as an act of betrayal of my own fellowship and to cause hurt and confusion among our people. Doubtless they also hoped to provoke a split in the ranks of our fellowship by enticing me and others to take the path of Judas.

Obviously I rejected the proposition and asked not to be visited again. One immediate result was that the KGB gave orders that I was to be taken out of the joinery and sent to fell trees in the forest, work that they could see was well beyond my health and strength. My overseer in the forest tried to help me by transferring me to the cook house, but when the camp authorities found out, I was ordered back to the tree-felling. Within nine months my health had deteriorated so badly and my heart had become so affected that the camp doctor released me from that heavy work.

*   *   *

On his release from that period of imprisonment, Nikolai Baturin was forced to go underground, because it seemed obvious that he would be quickly rearrested. However, during November 1979, the police found him and took him into custody. After a lengthy detention while investigations were carried out, he was sentenced to five years in a concentration camp.

During his initial detention, Pastor Baturin's health problems became so serious that the prison authorities responded to an inquiry with the terse statement, "He is still alive." Since Pastor Baturin has been in a concentration camp, letters have been very irregular, and it appears that he is to be denied visits until the end of his sentence. His sudden removal to an investigation prison led to a trial on new charges and an additional sentence that will last to the end of 1986.

When he was last at liberty, Pastor Baturin was asked if he had not grown tired and disillusioned after two decades of constant persecution. In reply he told of how, in 1962, hardly any young people in their teens and twenties attended the Baptist meetings in his hometown. As far as younger children were concerned, there were less than five. Even so, when he was being transported into exile a militia officer had punched him in the face and said, "This is for taking children with you to your meetings!"

However, when he was released in 1965, he found the number of younger children had increased to over thirty. By the time of his next release in 1969, there was a considerable body of teens and twenties. In fact, half the congregation by that time was composed of young people. After his release in 1976, the number of young people had grown to such an extent that the older brethren were a minority. "Therefore," he said, "our sufferings are not in vain in the Lord, and this thought always gives us renewed courage."

At the end of 1983 Pastor Baturin's wife was allowed to

visit him in the investigation prison, though she was only permitted to speak to him for ten minutes. Their conversation had to be conducted from separate cubicles connected by telephone. Shortly before the allotted time ran out Baturin suddenly gave some indication of new charges that had been leveled against him. Speaking rapidly, he said that he had been committed for investigation after two prisoners had professed conversion. He had been accused of "deliberately spreading false inventions" and threatened that if he told his wife anything more than that, he would be given a rough time. No sooner had Pastor Baturin spoken about these things than the conversation was terminated.

A trial was held in January 1984, when no less than thirteen witnesses were called to heap all kinds of slander upon him. Pastor Baturin discovered that the investigating magistrate had assured those witnesses that they need feel no sympathy for the one they slandered, for—"Baturin can no longer be helped. He is doomed to lifelong imprisonment. The next sentence will be followed by further sentences." So far, that is exactly what has occurred. After twenty years of imprisonment, Nikolai Baturin is a very tired man who should be particularly remembered in prayer by the Lord's people as he faces the coming ordeals.

14

A Drunken Doctor
Becomes an Imprisoned Pastor

Ivan Antonov is pastor of the unregistered Baptist congregation at Kirovograd, and he is also a member of the Council of Unregistered Baptist Churches. But until May 1987 he will be in a strict regime prison, and after that he will have to spend five years in internal exile, probably in some remote spot in the far north. This sentence is Pastor Antonov's fifth prison term. He is now aged sixty-five and is in failing health. What influences brought this former army doctor into the ranks of persecuted Baptist pastors? Here, Ivan Antonov traces his own experiences.

PASTOR ANTONOV'S STORY

I was born on August 19, 1919, in the village of Lipno, Bologodsky region, Kalinskaya district, where I spent my childhood and adolescence. Both my parents devoutly professed the Russian Orthodox faith, and my mother taught me to believe in God as a child. I entered the village school when I was six years old, and when I finished, I entered the high school at Medvedevo Station.

When I was twelve years old I had a dream. I dreamed that I was asleep on a grassy green meadow, with a bright blue sky above me and the sun rising in the East. Suddenly an angel (a pleasant old man) came and woke me up. I jumped up before him, and he laid his hand on my head saying, "Son, if you want to be a good person and study well, you must believe in God and pray." I awoke from my dream with both fear and excitement, and from that moment I began to believe in God and say my prayers according to the Russian Orthodox tradition, as I had been taught.

In 1938 I entered the Moscow Medical Institute to train as a doctor, though the war cut short my final year. I had hoped to find the meaning of life and personal fulfillment in science, but I was to be very disappointed. I first came across a Bible in the summer of 1941. With real desire and pleasure I read it through in a month and was greatly impressed. At that time, to my mother's dismay, I renounced icons, for I could no longer regard them as sacred.

In March 1942 I was drafted into the army, where I served at the front as a medical officer, going through great hardship of both body and soul. Although I had a strange, yet strong belief that I would not be wounded or killed, I drank heavily, and soon the sin of drunkenness completely enslaved me. There I was, a twenty-four-year-old army doctor struggling to conquer this most destructive vice, but I could do nothing to help myself.

A drinking buddy tried to kill me with a revolver on two occasions. Crushed and demoralized by my own sinful life, I no longer wanted to live, and I contemplated suicide. About that time I consulted a fortune-teller who at our first meeting told me about my past and predicted prison for the future, although she did not know that I would become a believer! Tempting me with talk of riches and money, she suggested that I study fortune-telling with her, but the very thought stirred within me a fear of God, and I began to pray again.

At that point, the month of June 1944, the merciful Lord answered my cries by causing me to meet some young Christian women. It was through the lives and conversation of those young women that I began to want to find Christ in a personal way. I became deeply ashamed of all my sins and began to grasp what Jesus Christ had done to pay the price of sin on the cross of Calvary. In earnest prayer I repented and received forgiveness and release from my sins.

Difficulties began immediately after my conversion, for I received mocking, threats, hostility, and goading from my colleagues, fellow officers, and seniors. But the Lord helped me to face up to all the trials and to speak to everyone about how I became a Christian. I also began to study the Bible and explain the way of salvation to many others. To my great happiness, a few soldiers sought and found the Lord for themselves. However, the number of accusations and threats against me increased and in November 1984, a military tribunal—which had at first threatened me with execution—sentenced me to ten years inprisonment.

I spent all my sentence, with the exception of three months, in the northern camps of Komi, ASSR, where I witnessed many atrocities. In answer to the prayers of many people my God was with me, protecting me from evil and giving me strength to witness to others about His love. What indescribable joy filled my heart when souls turned to the living God and found comfort in Him!

The authorities had begun proceedings to give me a further sentence for speaking about the gospel, but He to whom is given all power in heaven and earth changed everything. In August 1954, three months before my term was up, I was released. A month later, there in those northern waters, I was baptized by the pastor of a Baptist church. After that God gave me joyful reunions with my relatives in flesh and in spirit. I was married in 1955 to Lina* Korolkova, who had been sentenced in 1950 to twenty-five years imprisonment for working with young people but also for leading me, an officer, to the Lord. However, in June 1955 she was released. In the registered Baptist fellowship of Kirovograd I was trained to preach and was elected secretary to the preaching elders. I

*Lina is the familiar form of Neonila.

worked in a factory to support my family.

In our church we were required to have a government official serving as a member of the diaconate. He was appointed by the local Soviet Committee for Religious Affairs, and he attended all meetings of the diaconate and the church members. He regulated our affairs, and we met his demands.

At the beginning of the 1960s the interference of the government official in our congregation increased. He insisted, for example, that no baptisms should take place until he had first approved the list of candidates. If the list included young people, he would delete their names and order the list to be rewritten. As secretary of the preachers, I refused to exclude young people from the list, and for that I was dismissed from my office.

All the other preaching elders rose to defend and support the demands of the government official. Once he ordered our choir leader to be removed, and the church members tried every means of reinstating him, without success. I well remember how a special meeting of the membership was convened over this matter. A pastor named Andreyev, who was the senior pastor in the Ukraine and assistant to the chairman of the registered Baptist denomination, attended that meeting and justified the dismissal of the choir leader by quoting the Word of God in the book of Job, "The Lord gave and the Lord has taken away" [Job 1:21, NASB*]. He said, "The Lord, in His own time, gave us the choir leader who labored well, and now the Lord is removing him from this ministry." One elderly man present responded, "Not ' the Lord gave and the Lord has taken away,' but—' the Lord gave and Satan has taken away.' " Andreyev smoothed the protest over with a joke, and though the brethren vigorously defended our choir leader, it was all in vain.

A number of preachers and members in our district could not remain indifferent to the plight of the young people who

*New American Standard Bible.

were denied baptism, so we decided that we would preach about baptism and perform baptisms secretly. When our senior pastors became aware of it, they were very annoyed and threatened us with punishment, forbidding us to baptize young people anywhere. Nevertheless, we strove to hold to the Bible and to obey God in those matters.

Then things became even worse. In 1960 the registered Baptist denomination published and distributed to all churches an "Instructional Letter." It cut out all children's work, excluding them from all services and other meetings, banned young people's baptisms, forbade the use of visiting preachers from other churches and proscribed all conferences and fraternal gatherings. When I objected to the introduction of such documents into the churches, I was dismissed from ministering in any capacity, and later, along with other members, both men and women, I was excommunicated. Soon afterward I was accused of having committed criminal acts.

The KGB interviewed me and made several attempts—including the use of threats—to recruit me as an informer. When I refused they said, "You will never be an elder here in Kirovograd." However, contrary to their threats, I was again appointed to the pastoral ministry by an assembly of friends outside their influence and control.

At that time a number of Baptist preachers were taking the initiative to stir believers to take a more biblical stand. They had begun to send letters across the whole country, appealing for the cleansing of our churches. They called for the convening of a national conference of Baptist churches to come to grips with the situation. With joy and thanksgiving to God for their initiative our group responded to that call.

In 1962 I left my factory job, and for the next three years I carried out a ministry underground, preaching and undertaking various duties for our growing band of unregistered churches. Once, after a regular gathering of my own congregation, I was followed and detained by KGB agents. After three days they released me on the condition that I got a job.

They suggested that I work with them and they would make me a senior pastor, but I refused.

The worship services of our unofficial Baptist church at Kirovograd were continually disrupted by the militia. We were repeatedly fined, our Christian literature was confiscated, and we were summoned to the authorities for interrogation. The KGB constantly tried to recruit the leaders to work as informers and agents within the churches. Then in 1969 I was arrested and sentenced to serve three years in a strict regime prison camp. But God was with me, wonderfully protecting me and supplying all my needs.

A year after my release I was again threatened with imprisonment. Finding my ministry curtailed and aware that my freedom would be short-lived, I left my home and family in November 1972 to dedicate myself to the wider work of the Lord underground.

*   *   *

Since that time Pastor Antonov has been arrested and sentenced to prison terms three more times. His current sentence followed a trial in 1982, where he was charged with "violating the person and rights of citizens under the pretense of exercising religious observances." Pastors in his position are repeatedly interviewed by KGB officers making offers of release in exchange for collaboration as informers.

But men who truly know their Savior and who have frequently proved His companionship and power, stand true to their life's work. Dr. Antonov once wrote: "It is my desire to faithfully complete the ministry that I received from the Lord and the church, and to reach my heavenly home, where in the arms of eternal love we will enjoy fellowship with all the saints and those who love the Lord."

15
Trials of a Non-Collaborator

While there are sincere believers in many registered churches in Russia they are compelled, as we have noted, to accept severe restrictions on their activities and interference in their church government. The authorities will frequently choose the pastors, and they will be men who have agreed to accept the government's rules and give information on believers when called upon to do so.

The movement of unregistered churches is undoubtedly the most militant evangelical body in the Soviet Union, and consequently those churches suffer the main persecution. Their pastors go to prison, and their members suffer persecution as well because they refuse to curtail their witness. Their young people are put in concentration camps because they secretly print Bibles and other literature.

Pastor Pyotr Rumachik, now fifty-five, is one of the leading pastors among the two thousand unregistered Baptist churches. Prior to his current prison term, he had already spent eleven-and-a-half years in labor camps and exile, then he was forced to work underground to avoid rearrest by the KGB. In 1980 he was found and sentenced to five years imprisonment in a strict regime camp. Since that time he has been subjected to such terrible brutality that his health has been shattered. His prison visits have been canceled for long periods because he has been in no condition to be seen by members of his family. Following such a period, his wife was eventually granted a four-hour visit in October 1984. She reported that he was almost unrecognizable because he was so pale and thin. He appeared in the visiting room fitted with a catheter to drain an infection. He told Mrs. Rumachik, "My life is in God's hands." Doctors have since certified him to be suffering from coronary heart disease, chronic sinusitis, and inflammation of the gall bladder.

Despite his appalling physical condition Pastor Rumachik was sent back to work in the prison camp in early 1985. It soon became apparent that KGB officers were seeking grounds to extend his prison term, and shortly before his release date in August 1985 he was transferred to an investigation prison to face new charges. Here is Pastor Rumachik's own account of his conversion and commitment to the unregistered churches.

Pastor Rumachik's Story

I was born in 1931, and as my mother was a Christian believer, I heard about God from my childhood. However, I did not come to know the Lord for myself until I was seventeen. My conversion brought me to trust and love my Savior, and I sought to serve Him in whatever way possible. The years 1955-1960 are especially memorable for me. While in the Podmoskve fellowship of Dedovsk (a suburb of Moscow), I actively participated in the pioneer stages of a local church. At that time I preached and later served on the church diaconate.

During that time it became obvious to many of us that representatives of the official denomination of registered Baptists were not loyal to the fellowship and were actually working toward tearing down the churches. That naturally affected our fellowship, although it had only recently been organized and had not formally entered the denomination. Nevertheless, denominational workers tried to exert their influence on us, attempting to stop the development of our young church. Although during that period we did not encounter any particular obstruction on the part of the local Soviet authorities, we were confronted with much obstruction by the denominational officials.

With every possible admonition, they asked us to dismiss and dismantle our church, which would have meant that in the area of Dedovsk the witness for Christ would be liquidated. It was apparent that the denomination (or government organs working through it) was not prepared to permit a church in the Moscow area where believers could find true and free service to God, independent from the government. We saw that such work of the official denomination of registered Baptists contradicted the Word of God, and we could not comply with their demands. Soon the persecution began. Over a period of two years many brethren, including me, were repeatedly arrested and fined. House searches began, and preachers were accused of criminal acts.

We were charged with beginning a church in Dedovsk, conducting meetings at the home of Vasili Yakovlevich Smirnov, organizing the participation of youth and children in the church, and committing insubordination to the registered denomination. In September 1961, five preachers from our church, including me, were sentenced and exiled to Krasnoyarsky kray. Among the convicting evidence was a document about us by the senior pastor of the official Baptist denomination in the Moscow area, Pastor A. N. Karpov. His document was the indictment by which the official denomination gave its consent to our conviction.

God's mercies never deserted me in that lonely wilderness exile. It was possible to work for His glory there too. Although deprived of all possible comforts, God's help and the joy of seeing new converts were truly rewards from Him. During my exile many welcome changes occurred in the brotherhood of evangelical Baptists. An action group was organized, which exposed our denomination's departure from truth and called us to petition for a congress of all Baptists.

However, the Soviet authorities and the denominational leadership did everything possible to resist God's people in this effort. All the supporters of the new initiative endured the disruption of their worship services. Their church buildings were confiscated or demolished, and the pastors and deacons received imprisonment or fines.

But these revived churches moved resolutely ahead on the narrow path and boldly carried the light of the gospel to people around them. Time passed, and the Lord carried on His work. By the prayers of many of God's children, prisoners were being released with complete rehabilitation. In August 1965, I too was released and rehabilitated. Some of the confiscated private homes in which services had been held were returned to their owners. However, in our church, that part of the house that the judge had taken away from Vasili Smirnov four years previously was not returned. Indeed, the rest of the house was confiscated, and thus it became obvious to us that the local authorities and the official Baptist denomination did not want a dynamic fellowship in the Dedovsk area.

I resumed my preaching work in my fellowship, and in 1966 I was chosen and ordained an evangelist by the church. Our meetings were held in the private homes of people who, despite repression, wanted to see the Dedovsk fellowship prosper. However, it was a very difficult period, as a new wave of repression lashed at believers across the country.

In 1966 many churches like ours sent delegates to Moscow to petition for the granting of religious freedom and an end to the repression. However, the delegation was arrested, and I was one of those sentenced to a fourteen-day imprisonment. Upon returning home, I discovered that several leaders of our action group had also been arrested. They included Gennadi Kryuchkov and Georgi Vins. The wave of repression grew, but God's children carried on, rejoicing in the sorrows and praising God for their lot.

The persecution did not spare the Dedovsk church. The authorities constantly tormented the church, disrupting worship services, confiscating spiritual literature, and conducting house searches. Very soon the Lord called me to again be a prisoner in His name. I was arrested and in June 1968 sentenced to three years imprisonment. I served only half of that sentence because of an amnesty.

I returned to my church, where the members were still experiencing great persecution. Immediately the authorities began summoning me and warning that if I did not curtail my religious activities I would be imprisoned again. Just the same, I tried to serve the Lord faithfully. At the end of 1969 a conference of ministers from our new brotherhood of churches was held in Tula, and I was present. Representatives from numerous churches approved the work that had been accomplished in the face of persecution and sorrows during the period 1961-1969. I was one of those chosen for the Council board, although I was unable to serve in that capacity because I was again arrested and imprisoned in Volokolamskaya prison. Here the KGB tried to persuade me to work with them.

On one occasion two KGB workers came to talk with me for almost five hours. First they told me that I was convicted of breaking the laws governing religion, but then they changed their tactics and said they did not consider me to be a criminal. They told me about my family, that they had seen my wife and children who were enjoying a wonderful life in freedom. They reminded me that I too could live in freedom like others. Then they came to direct bargaining. One of them offered me freedom in exchange for collaborating with the KGB. "We will make you a minister in any church near Moscow," he added.

"But I know that the believers themselves choose their ministers," I protested. But he insisted that everything would be arranged, and they could appoint me the minister through the believers. Then I said to them, "All along you have been trying to convince me that you do not interfere in church affairs. How then can you make such a proposal as this to me? With this attempt to enlist me as a KGB helper you have canceled all your assertions of noninterference in church affairs. Besides, I am not Judas that I would be a traitor for thirty pieces of silver."

With that the discussion ended, but the KGB officers reminded me as they left that if I should want to meet with them, they would be ready to help me at any time. And so new trials for the Lord's name began. This time I was sentenced to three years strict regime camp and sent to the Urals to work in the forests. In January 1973 I was freed. I left behind me the zones, the convoy, the barbed wire, and once again there was a joyful reunion with my family and church. Grateful to God, I continued work in the Lord's vineyard, but all too soon there were new threats, new fines, and new persecutions. The powers of this world had not changed their attitude to the persecuted brotherhood, nor especially to the ministers.

The ministry of the council of churches was becoming increasingly complex. Several leading brethren had already been forced to carry out their work secretly. However, God's cause was growing in scope and strength. Evangelists were preaching the gospel to the unsaved; the secret printing presses that we had started continued to operate; the Council of Prisoners' Relatives encouraged the prisoners with intercession and family support work. But I was not free for long. In 1974 I was yet again sentenced to three years strict regime prison camp. All over again I experienced the transportation, transit prisons, the inhumane overcrowding, and the rowdiness and cursing of the prisoners.

During the trial, efforts had been made repeatedly to draw me into collaboration with the atheists. In exchange they offered me sweet freedom. The senior examining magistrate did not sit alone in my pretrial examination. Once (as is common during interrogation) I was taken to the militia department, where a certain Mikhail Mikhailovich Miroshin introduced himself. Apparently he was one of the officials concerned with religious questions in our region. His part in my trial was obvious, for he gave orders to the examining magistrate regarding how my case was to be handled and what charges should be brought against me. On the table in front of him was literature in Russian and foreign languages.

He gave me a piece of literature to look at. On the cover was a picture of a rising or setting sun, barbed wire, a guard with a bayonet, and from behind the barbed wire were hands, reaching to the sun as though to freedom, and the inscription: "Martyrs for Christ in the USSR." Miroshin made clear to me that this literature was published abroad and emphasized that he and others did not want such literature to be published.

I answered him directly, saying that it was pointless talking to me about that, because it did not depend on me, but on him and others like him. "If you stop the persecution of believers," I said, "such literature won't be printed. If there is no persecution, there will be nothing to write about. So you see, the resolution is in your hands, not ours."

In that conversation he also suggested that I was being prosecuted for breaking the laws governing separation of church and state. He tried to prove that the viewpoint of the Council of Unregistered Churches was erroneous, and by various tactics he tried to convince me to influence the brethren on the council to change their position.

"But how could I possibly help you, or influence anyone, under my present conditions? I am in prison," I reminded him. Then he made it clear that if I were to consent, I might be freed. It was perfectly obvious that I would not consent, and I plainly stated that the attitude of our council's ministers was based on irrefutable facts. Persecution for faith in God was taking place in our country; homes were being taken away from believers; worship services were being disrupted; trials of believers were taking place; and heavy penalties were being imposed.

During the trial proceedings, I discovered that two experts had been called in. One was a man named Garkavenko, a philosophy academic, and the other man was named Lialina, an educationalist. They were supposed to provide an objective religious assessment of the literature that had been taken from me. I made submissions to the effect that they, as atheists, had no theological training and were therefore unable to make an objective analysis. Nevertheless, in spite of my arguments these experts took part in my trial, and my eventual conviction was based entirely on the evidence that their expertise provided.

I was allowed three days to acquaint myself with the evidence. On the third day Garkavenko, one of the experts, came to speak to me personally. During our discussion he tried to bully me, saying that our council of churches incited people to make appeals to the authorities with various demands. Thus it was the council that initiated discontent.

"So you see," he said, "you may yet have to pay very dearly for this. If some form of unfavorable circumstances came about in our country, you could be stood up against a wall and shot." To conclude our discussion he said: "Watch out! If you don't work with us, it is in our power to ease or harden your situation upon your arrival at the prison camp."

This time I was sentenced to three years, and I spent them at the same camp that I had been in for my previous sentence. There again I prayed that I might be used by God in the camp and spent much time answering the questions of the prisoners and telling them about the Lord. And so between 1961 and 1977 I was sentenced four times for a total of fourteen years for serving the Lord. Of the fourteen years, I spent eleven-and-one-half years in camps and exile.

That is, of course, insignificant in the light of what the apostle Paul said: "Ye have not yet resisted unto blood, striving against sin" [Hebrews 12:4]. But whatever the Lord has predestined for me in the future, whether suffering or death for His sake, need not frighten me, because a glorious eternity awaits me that I would not exchange for anything in this life. That glorious eternity has always attracted, and still attracts, all the pilgrims on this present, narrow, thorny, sorrowful path. With Paul, I want to say of suffering, "But none of these things move me, neither count I my life dear unto myself, so that I might finish my course with joy, and the ministry, which I have received of the Lord Jesus" (Acts 20:24).

16

Determined to Silence the Leading Pastors

Pastor Dmitri Minyakov is a sixty-five-year-old widower who was released from a five-year sentence in January 1986. Most of this was spent in a strict regime concentration camp in Kuybyshev. He a member of the Council of Unregistered Baptist Churches and has served a total of twelve years in prisons and labor camps. This is the life of Pastor Minyakov told in his own words and concluding with his account of the cruel victimization to which he was subjected in his most recent imprisonment. This is an example of the particularly brutal treatment meted out to the leading ministers of the unregistered church movement.

Pastor Minyakov's Story

I met Christians for the first time at the beginning of a prison term I was serving from 1944 until 1952. I remember how Christian prisoners were mocked and taunted. Yet I experienced a decisive conversion to the Lord in 1949, and I was baptized by Baptist fellow prisoners right there in the concentration camp. The Christians in our camp managed to get together for services. We even had a pastor, but he was later transferred to another camp, so in 1950 I was appointed by the fellowship to lead our services.

On my release I settled in the town of Mariinsk, Kemerovskoi oblast, where I continued to serve as a lay preacher. We had great blessing in our church, and in a single year fifteen people experienced true repentance and conversion. At the end of the 1950s, my wife and I moved to Barnaul, where I became secretary of the Evangelical Baptist Church and a preacher. Despite restrictions, young people tried to get together for Bible studies. At that time the congregation felt compelled to expel the pastor for his departure from the truth. However, because he was collaborating with the authorities, they closed our meeting place. We then began meeting in homes, and I was chosen to be pastor. The ministry was complicated, and times were difficult. Most churches were being pastored by men like our expelled minister.

Then in 1961 a brother came from Novosibirsk with a circular letter from an action group of pastors who wanted to lift the churches out of the trap of compromise. I read the letter in a meeting and could hardly restrain myself from crying. I could sense in that letter the same concern that I felt for God's people who had departed from the truth and the same anguish for the work that filled my own heart. It seemed to me that God Himself had put on paper exactly what was troubling me. Our church immediately joined in petitioning for a Congress of Evangelical Baptist Churches.

Gennadi Kryuchkov came up to Siberia to see us. I remember how our group of Siberians listened to him. For two hours he spoke to us about the apostasy of the official Baptist denominational workers, and he called us to faithfulness to our God. That message was so real and near to our hearts! I had been upset about the apostasy and dishonesty prevalent in our churches and had seen no way out of the situation, but when God opened the veil and indicated this solution, I rejoiced and praised Him. The believers in Siberia chose me to serve on the steering committee for the Congress of Unregistered Baptist Churches. Even then we knew that the path would be thorny, but to go any other way would mean denying the Word of God.

In 1962 I was arrested for my part in the unregistered church movement and then sentenced to five years imprisonment with confiscation of all my property. The trial was a travesty of justice. Constant slander in films, radio, and newspapers had incited such hatred against Baptist "fanatics" that the angry crowd at the trial was ready to tear us to pieces. I passed through about twelve prisons and concentration camps in the period between 1962 and 1965. I became seriously ill for most of the time and did not expect to survive, but God was merciful. Upon my release I again began to work for the Lord, so that in 1966 I was put on the wanted list. That was the same year that a delegation of believers from many churches throughout the country went to Moscow to petition for an end to persecution. At the Central Committee of the Communist Party building they were beaten and arrested. Then the persecution of believers intensified radically. After two years of liberty I was arrested again and sentenced to three years imprisonment. During that time I passed through eighteen prisons and concentration camps and again suffered very poor health.

In 1974 I took my family to live in the Baltic area. I bought a house in the village of Ligantna, but the court annulled my sale contract in order to expel me from the area, and so we were forced to move to Valga in Estonia. As soon as we had moved, the KGB began interviewing me. They threatened me and tried to persuade me to abandon my work on the Council of Unregistered Baptist Churches. On one occasion they raided our house, breaking windows and ransacking the rooms. They took a transistor radio, wristwatch, cassette tapes, and more than three thousand rubles. On another occasion our youngest son came running into our bedroom in the middle of the night saying that two men were looking in through the window. My wife and I got dressed and went outside. At the end of our garden we saw a car. The driver turned out to be a major in the KGB in the town of Valga.

Once when my wife and I went to visit our son who was serving in the army, eight men were sent to search our house. They got my eldest son from work, entered the house, and took all the Christian literature and other materials they could find. They took personal possessions: cassette tapes, photographs, films, a typewriter, family albums, and personal correspondence from relatives and friends covering ten years.

However, I thank my God that during the seventeen-year battle for the rebirth and revival of an uncompromised Baptist witness and through all the years of persecution, I have never doubted the rightness of this path. I want to accept gladly whatever the Lord permits to take place. I pray above all for strength to remain faithful to Him and to lay down my life for my brethren and the work that God is doing in our country.

*   *   *

Towards the end of 1980, "wanted" posters appeared at police offices and railway stations everywhere bearing pictures of Pastor Minyakov. The general public normally associates such posters with notorious criminals. Pastor Minyakov's poster carried these words in Estonian and Russian: "Wanted! Citizens—we are searching for ex-convict Minyakov Dmitri Vasilievich, born 1921, who has been sentenced several times previously and has again committed offenses. He is evading the investigating authorities. The police will be grateful to anyone who can give information as to the whereabouts of this man."

Within a matter of months Dmitri Minyakov was caught. He was arrested at a road check-point at Rostov-on-Don in January 1981 and held for seven months before his trial took place in the city of Tallinn, Estonia. He was sentenced to five years in a strict regime labor camp and ordered to suffer the confiscation of all his personal property, his home, furniture, and even personal effects. At the trial, only his relatives were allowed to witness the proceedings, and even they were only admitted because Pastor Minyakov refused to speak until they were present.

Pastor Minyakov was originally charged with having betrayed his country—an offense that could carry a sentence of up to fifteen years imprisonment. Probably as the result of Western concern that charge was withdrawn, and the pastor was sentenced for his religious activities. The court also held him guilty of raising his own children to become Christians. Pastor Minyakov suffers from a very severe form of asthma and felt that he might not survive this further period of imprisonment. Within a year his condition became serious, and he wrote home from a concentration camp on the River Optar, describing his health problem in these words:

> The worst thing about it is that the doctors cannot do a thing for it. After taking tablets or having injections the difficulty in breathing eases for two or three hours, but then the attacks become more violent, as if the asthma is taking revenge for being treated. I have been suffering for weeks like this. In addition, I have fits of coughing severe enough to make me sick. A great deal of phlegm is produced—up to half a liter a day. That is how I now live. What is bad is that everything inside is so inflamed by this continual, heart-rending coughing that you cannot hold your body because every touch causes pain. The doctor told me that this asthma is of a particular kind because the attacks last for up to three weeks and begin again after a pause of one week.

The recent trials of this pastor have included the most inhumane treatment possible, as this letter from Kuybyshev shows:

> This year I have been in the camp sick bay three times, in the prison hospital four times, and for months I have lain in the barracks unable to get to either the sick bay or to roll call because of my asthma. The asthma attacks usually last about three weeks. Just as I am recovering from one attack, another begins. I choke almost without a break. In addition I have chronic bronchitis and tuberculosis.
> This "bouquet," as the doctors call it, is helping the asthma to bring me to a speedy end. I also have constant pain from my heart and kidneys, and from bleeding hemor-

rhoids. From March 19 to May 10 I was in hospital but came out no better than when I was admitted. On May 14 I was taken to the Central Hospital, but I asked to be taken back to the camp hospital because I became worse there. At least I can breathe some fresh air in the concentration camp, even though there is only a small courtyard and people smoke constantly.

On May 25 Major Samoshkin, the acting head of political education at the camp, unexpectedly asked me, "Minyakov, why did you not turn up for work today? I warn you, if you do not go to work tomorrow you'll have trouble!"

So on May 26 I was forced to go to work. I had to make nets. My hands were shaking and everything was swimming before my eyes. The threads leapt around in my field of vision. I have never woven nets before, and I got a headache from the sheer exertion. I did not manage to make a single net. I had nothing to show for my efforts by the evening. I was then thrown into the punishment block, where there was no air. There were about twenty men in there —all young men apart from me. Half an hour went by, a whole hour, and the sweat was running off us.

The men began to pound on the door demanding air. The guards opened the observation hole and sprayed tear gas into the cell. I pressed myself to the ground to get some air, prayed, and prepared to die. The gas took my breath away, and I was close to suffocation. The next day I went to the camp commandant and told him of my condition and what had happened in the punishment cell. He arranged for me to be left in peace for the whole of June.

On July 4, Samoshkin had me put back in the punishment cell for failing to go to work. I had to stay there an entire day. I was also forbidden to buy anything in the camp shop for a month. On July 5 I was put in the punishment cell again, this time from 10:00 A.M. until 10:00 P.M. The same happened on July 7. The cell was packed with prisoners, and air only came into the cell at times when the double doors were opened.

The air was terribly bad, and the whole situation was made worse because there was no toilet—not even a bucket—in the cell. There were puddles of urine on the floor that had been sprinkled over with powdered bleach. In addition, men were smoking. The young men were only kept in the cell for a few hours. On July 5 I was the only prisoner to be kept there for the whole day without food. I felt so poisoned that I could scarcely drag myself into bed that evening.

Since I had not gone to work on July 5 I was struck off the list of those allowed to receive visitors. And because I was not allowed to buy anything in the camp shop, my only opportunity to eat anything fit for a human being was taken from me. From the camp shop I would at least have bought some simple sweets and eaten them with boiled water. On July 6 I was collected from the punishment block and taken to the camp hospital. The doctors declared me unfit but said that the Central Hospital had classified me as a grade-three invalid, and in that category one still has to go to work. As the camp doctors are subordinate in rank to those in the Central Hospital, they could not alter that. Age is not considered in concentration camps.

The camp commandant, Major Valayev, was right when, on November 11, 1983, he said to Major Koshmetyev in my presence, "We had a painter and he was killed, now there is a saint left. It's possible that he too will die before long." It is noticeable that the deaths that occur take place in the work areas. It is said by the prisoners that the most favorable conditions for murder are packing areas, workshops, garages, building sites, and trenches. If I am deprived of all my rights in the camp, then my fate is sealed in the punishment cell. With every hour I melt down more and more. Another three or four days in the punishment cell under the conditions I have described and I will not be able to walk any more. After ten to fifteen days in the punishment cell I will be finished.

In spite of all, do not be sad, my precious children. If the Lord permits it, then I shall be going to Him, for I have not offended the nation, nor the government, nor Valayev, nor anyone else on this earth. I will go to heaven at the time the Lord has determined with a clear conscience. I am tortured for His sake, and I shall go on speaking of Him.

Towards the end of 1985 Pastor Minyakov was taken from the prison camp to a regional hospital where it was confirmed that he was suffering from pulmonary tuberculosis and possibly a malignant tumor. He was told that the Soviet Red Cross had intervened, a clear indication that many Christians have written to the Red Cross on his behalf. Minyakov's release in January 1986 came as a surprize to observers in the West, in view of the tendency for leading pastors to be given new prison terms before their sentences have expired. At an emotional homecoming service, Pastor Minyakov told of how numerous prisoners had listened to his words of witness over the years, and of the comfort he had derived from the enormous number of letters he had received. How greatly such leading pastors need the sustaining prayers of Christians everywhere as they endure the sufferings because they are obedient to the Word of God.

17

Evangelism and Church Life Among the Baptists

The author of this chapter is Hermann Hartfeld, a formerly imprisoned pastor who is now in the West. He explains the evangelical methods of the persecuted churches and how they govern their congregations:

The evangelistic approaches that are taken up among Christians in the Soviet Union are very different from those in the West, partly because of the different culture and partly because the Russian churches are compelled to use unusual methods. The first feature of our evangelistic approach in the Soviet Union is to emphasize the fact that evangelism affects every area of each individual believer's life. Wherever you go and whatever you do, you must never forget that you are a child of God and that you must shine out the grace of Jesus Christ that you have experienced. In our churches, every Christian is challenged to be a faithful witness in every part of his life.

Believers challenge themselves concerning all the occupations and activities in which they have been involved in their lives, asking, How will this help my witness? How will it help my church or the spiritual life of my family? Will it do any spiritual good? Alongside the work of personal witness, the elders and lay preachers in our churches try to deliver at least one evangelistic message every week. That is regarded as highly important. Our worship services usually last two to three hours, and during those services, not one preacher but generally two or three give addresses. One of those preachers must give an evangelistic sermon.

In addition to that public ministry, Russian Christians conduct rallies held in the mountains and forests. As you may know, Russian youth is extremely energetic. The Russian people are very impulsive and emotional, and the young people are usually intensely dynamic. They like to have their own meetings. They try to invite their unbelieving friends to such rallies, and there are times when they gather as many as 1,200 young people to hear an evangelistic message. At least once a year they hold a conference somewhere in the mountains in the hope that the KGB will not find them, although they usually do.

Evangelistic activities are also conducted during weddings. In Russia we invite many people to our weddings. A believing couple may invite as many as two thousand people. I did not have a lot of money and could invite only four hundred people to my wedding. I invited many people from my factory, and my wife did the same. Pastor Skornyakov officiated and delivered an evangelistic message in which he sought to show the people what marriage actually means and that to have a truly stable married life, people must have Jesus Christ as their Lord and Savior.

We also have birthday parties for evangelistic purposes. It is important to invite to your birthday party many unbelievers. As can be imagined, when a church has 120 members, there can be a birthday party every few days! Many friends who are unbelievers will be invited, and there will be an opportunity to deliver a beautiful evangelistic message.

Funerals are also an opportunity to reach others, because large numbers gather at funerals. A former evangelist in our churches, now in the West, specialized in speaking at funerals. He said to me, "I could hardly wait for someone to die." He would be invited to many different areas to preach at funerals, and for that reason he was indicted and put into prison.

When someone dies in a village, the whole population will gather at the cemetery and listen to what is said. The speaker will tell them that we hold regular worship services in private houses. He will say that we are not an underground church but a persecuted church, that we are hated, and we do not know why. He will tell them that the authorities hate us, but we do not know why, except perhaps that we love the Lord. "Look at us," he will say. "We are not thieves; we are not adulterers—look at our life-style. We are ordinary people, and you are welcome at our worship services."

Once a preacher or any other believer is arrested and put into a concentration camp, he has further opportunity to evangelize. He serves the prisoners. When I was released from prison in 1965, the criminals I was with cried out loud and told me that they would pray to God to send another Christian to their camp to minister to them.

Many prisoners become Christians through the testimony of imprisoned believers. Gennadi Kryuchkov, chairman of the Council of Evangelical Baptist Churches, once said that he will not find rest until everyone in the Soviet Union has heard the message of Jesus Christ. That is not solely the desire of Gennadi Kryuchkov but of all our people in Russia.

Our elders are similar to pastors in Western countries. We do not have the term "pastor," but we use the term "presbyter." Presbyters have the same responsibility and function in the same way as a pastor in Western countries. Some churches have a pastor, elders, and deacons, but that is not the case in Russia. A presbyter is usually ordained, but only after he has been tested by serving in that position for two or three years. During that time it will be seen if he possesses the right abilities and whether he is actually called to that ministry.

The pastor must be a dedicated Christian, an uncompromising child of God. If he does not show that, then he cannot be ordained. The office of pastor is a highly vulnerable position in Russian churches.

I knew a man who was a pastor in the city of Omsk,

where I studied agricultural machinery. He had been sentenced to five years imprisonment, and after completing this term he was released. Immediately the KGB tried to recruit him as one of their agents. The pastor refused. But in a very sly way they tried to persuade him that he need not inform them about his worship services or about his own activities, but only about the guests who visit his church. If he did that he would have complete freedom to conduct his worship services in any private house or anywhere else. The pastor still refused, so he was in freedom only three months before the KGB made an indictment against him, and he was put in labor camps again for five years. That was Pastor Sigirov, and his experience has been the experience of many others.

If the pastor is not unusually dedicated, he cannot be a pastor at all. Therefore it is necessary for our pastors to be thoroughly tested. The pastor must be dedicated to the Lord, a man of God who manages his own household well. He must have children who are Christians, and he must love the church and the Lord more than his own life. To us in Russia the functions of the pastor are as written in 1 Peter 5:2. It is their responsibility to ''feed the flock of God.''

I must confess that such an obligation has never been easy for a Russian pastor, because for many decades we did not have access to the Word of God. How can men teach when they have no Bibles? It is much easier to teach sound doctrine when there are Bibles and good commentaries available, but we have had times when pastors did not have anything. I remember when I was a member of a church in which we had only one Bible for one hundred members! It has changed in recent times—I must emphasize that as well.* But there was a time when an elder could only teach the tradition of his fathers, and according to those traditions he taught us to live. Sometimes the teaching inclined to legalism, but as soon as we had access to the Bible such things changed.

To teach sound doctrine is always a very responsible

---

*Because of the work of the underground presses.

task, especially in a country where one has to fight and battle with atheistic propaganda, as well as many sects, which are plentiful in Russia. The pastor must be a watchman for the whole church, so that no one falls into the trap of false teachers. In recent times the Council of Evangelical Baptist Churches has organized many Bible courses in local churches, designed for preachers to help them study and preach the Bible.

One of the men engaged in the training of men is Pastor Khabysh, who was recently arrested for his activities. He needs our prayers because his health is not very good. We should assist such activities by sending more literature to help the young preachers.

The elders also have the responsibility to organize, along with the youth leaders, those youth rallies and meetings in mountains and forests or other deserted places. As I have indicated already, such meetings are very important for us. Also the elders have the responsibility to oversee the Sunday school work. When I served with Pastor Khrapov, our ministry was very much blessed by the Lord. We had many, many teenagers who became Christians and who are now grown up and are very beautiful Christians.

Concerning discipline, I do not know much about the discipline that is exerted here in Western churches. I can only say that I have met with many churches that do not seem to exert any discipline at all. For us that is a strange thing because we exert discipline in Russia. Our churches would never tolerate an unrepentant adulterer, and we would in many circumstances excommunicate people for divorce. Obviously we would strive to avert such problems by our counseling.

The deacons are elected to be responsible for the social welfare work in the church. They are to care for the needs of widows, orphans, and those whose relatives are in the labor camps. That ministry is very much endangered by the fact that the Soviet law prohibits the churches from giving any financial assistance to anyone.

Our deacons therefore perform a very dangerous ministry. When the pastor is in prison they must take his place and carry on the services of the church. In addition to pastors and deacons we have youth leaders. The ministry to youth is the most dangerous ministry we engage in at local church level because all the power of the Soviet authorities is directed against the work among young people. When action is taken against a church, the first people to be arrested are usually the young people's leaders. So the youth leaders must be dynamic, energetic young people, dedicated to the Lord and able to take all the consequences of their ministry, even if it costs their freedom and lives.

Though our Russian congregations are well aware of many deficiencies and needs, they exhibit many qualities that should serve to encourage and challenge believers in other lands. The uncompromising service of suffering Christians to our Lord and Savior not only moves the hearts of believers, but it also impresses the enemies of the gospel. Furthermore, the Russian attitude to evangelism is a wonderful example of how ways may be found to proclaim the gospel message in many different cultural settings and circumstances.

Another lesson to be learned from the suffering churches arises from their attitude to the state. Christians in other parts of the world have sometimes become too involved in politics, and that involvement has distracted them from the primary purpose of bringing glory to our Lord Jesus Christ by fulfilling the great commission. Believers in the unregistered churches are not in favor of exclusiveness and "ghetto mentality," but they believe that the churches should abstain from political involvement, except, of course, that they believe in showing personal compassion and engaging in relief work.

Finally, the suffering churches teach us that imprisonments, demolition of churches, confiscation of Bibles, and all other intimidations and harassments will never destroy the love of God and the freedom that burns in the hearts of believers. They will triumph over any hostile power in the world.

18
The Drive Against Faith Among the Young

The Soviet state is determined to extinguish all religious influences on the rising generation, a fact that is evident from the renewed spate of militant speeches and legislation. Evidence of hardening attitudes is also seen in an increase in renewed reports of parents being threatened with the loss of their parental rights, a measure that had been laid aside in recent years. Loss of parental rights means that the children are placed in state children's homes for their "safety and education," and once there, parents are not even permitted to visit them.

It is not generally appreciated in the West just how vigorously the Soviet authorities pursue the campaign against faith among young people. Soviet law has prohibited the teaching of religion in schools and colleges since the revolution, but in more modern times (1961) laws were passed that required both schools and parents to train up children according to the moral code of communism. They are to be taught to show dedication to the communist cause and to maintain implacable hostility to the opponents of communism.

Still more recently (April 1984) tough new school guidelines have been introduced that give teachers the responsibility of policing parents who are indifferent to their communist duty, especially those who teach their children to believe in God. Such parents must be "strictly brought to account." A small quotation from this piece of legislation will show just what the authorities are determined to achieve.

> The entire rearing and educating of our youth must be a training in communist morals. . . . Schools must build up the child's inner need to live and act in harmony with the principles of communist morals and to adhere strictly to the rules of socialist community life and Soviet law. The unchangeable aim of communist education is the formation of their Marxist-Leninist world view. This depends on arts subjects, as well as science subjects, being so taught as to continuously mold the minds of pupils to understand rationalistic concepts, imparting to them the ability to explain the phenomena of nature, and to act in accordance with the principles of our world view.

In 1984 the Central Committee of the Communist Party emphasized how vital it was to eradicate belief in God among school-age youngsters, saying, "All means are now being deployed in the war on faith." At the same time the committee acknowledged that all efforts had not yet achieved the desired goal, and still greater efforts were called for.

The kind of pressure that may at any time be brought to bear upon Christian parents is to be seen in the case of Mrs. Tsybulskaya, a mother of four children from the village of Dubievka. While she was in the hospital, the local school gave her son Mikhail a red star with Lenin's image. Thus he became an "October Child"—a member of the communist organization for children.

On her return home Mrs. Tsybulskaya explained to her son that children of believers should not wear the star. She then explained their position to his teacher and asked her not to press the boy to wear it. The teacher replied, "I cannot agree to your request and will tell the headmaster of this conversation." Mrs. Tsybulskaya, whose husband is an invalid, was duly summoned to see the headmaster and told, "Because you do not recognize the star, and oppose the policy, we will bring you to account before the court."

A session of the village Soviet was duly convened, and Mrs. Tsybulskaya was accused of educating her children in the spirit of religion and of thus "mutilating" their understanding. Various warnings were given, and the child was required to wear the red star on return to school, though he refused. Up to now it is not known what further action has been taken, but the parents have appealed for prayer, and their experience has been duplicated in other places.

In past years the threat to take children from their parents was made with great frequency, but widespread publicity given in the West to certain prominent cases in the mid 1970s led to an abatement of such threats. However, in the last five years several cases have been reported where courts have made custody orders against believers. In October 1981, for example, Zinaida Mazunova of Shchekino lost custody of her thirteen-year-old adopted boy, Mikhail, because she was deemed incapable of bringing him up in accordance with the communist moral code as required by the marriage and family laws. The court decision specifically stated that her incapability arose from the fact that she was a believer.

Another case is that of Yevdokia Chooru of Kishinev who was deprived of her children when she was converted to Christ from alcoholism. In her case the authorities took advantage of a divorce action to deprive her of the custody of her children. Mrs. Chooru recorded her spiritual experience in these words:

> Until 1980 my life was lost in sin. I was especially afflicted with the vice of drinking. I fought it vigorously for I wanted to be free of it, but I could not give it up. I was treated for alcoholism in a psychiatric hospital, and then my husband sent me to an institution for alcoholics in Kharkov.
>
> My condition was very serious. Then I met a believing woman at work from whose lips I heard the message of the love and sufferings of Christ. I went to the believers' meetings and heard the Word of God. The Holy Spirit touched my heart, and I repented of my sin and believed in Jesus Christ as the only Savior.

Mrs. Chooru tells of how her husband would frequently return home drunk and then beat her in the sight of their children. However, in 1982 the court granted Mr. Chooru a divorce and also gave him the custody of the children, as he had found another woman who would educate them. The court ruled that Mrs. Chooru would only be permitted to have her children back if she renounced her religious beliefs.

The drive to stamp out faith in God among young people includes heavy penalties on any who develop too great an interest in religion. Teenagers are aware that as believers they will throw away all opportunities for a university education or for a good level of employment. Young believers know that if they do not join the Communist youth organization or participate in social dances and so on, those matters will be noted in their final school testimonials along with the fatal stigma—"This person is a believer." That will be enough to prevent acceptance to a good job or a college.

Tatyana Karpova is a working girl who sought admission to university, and her employer—a college—supplied a testimonial guaranteed to lead to rejection. It read:

> Comrade Karpova has been working in the State Technical College in Kishinev as a technician in the Department for Social Hygiene. In the course of time it emerged that Comrade Karpova is a member of the Baptist sect. Although she has taken part in the schooling system for party education and despite much effort by communist workers and department members to enlighten her, she still holds to her religious convictions.

If a young believer does manage to get to college (perhaps a technical college, but never a university), or if someone is converted while at college, it is highly unlikely that a graduation certificate will be awarded. A believing student named Kurnosov from Dubrovino had completed in five years the arduous and advanced agricultural course of the Leningrad College of Agriculture when he was dismissed because he had not passed the state examination in the subject of Scientific Communism. His work reference sent to the college stated: "From the viewpoint of materialistic theory, he is unworthy to possess the diploma of a Soviet engineer."

Yevgeni Meged studied at the College of Electronics in Ordzhonikidze. Like all other students he underwent a practical test before his final examinations. However, because he did not include a report on his political activities, and because he was not a member of Komsomol or a political activist, it was explained to him that he would not be admitted to the exams.

Galina Mashnitskaya, aged eighteen, is the daughter of Christian parents. She realized that it was pointless to press for a career of any significance because her father, Nikolai Mashnitsky, had twice been imprisoned for his active service in an unregistered church. Her mother had to visit the education department five times before Galina, classed as "the daughter of a sect member," was allowed to enroll at a school. Galina took a vocational course for training as a typist while at school. That work suited her, and after leaving school she found a job as a typist in a factory. Within two days she was dismissed on the grounds that she was too inexperienced.

On the advice of the job center, Galina applied to a road construction firm. The head of the personnel division soon ascertained that she was a believer and stated that she could start work on the following Monday. When, however, Galina appeared on that day, she discovered that he had hired another typist and did not need her. She was later dismissed from another firm on the grounds that she was too young. The employment exchange sent her to the education authority, where she worked for half a day until she was again dismissed for being too young. Eventually Galina's mother appealed to Mrs. Burko, secretary to the town council, asking her to help her daughter find a job. She advised her to see Comrade Yavorsky at the employment exchange.

From there Galina was sent to the regional committee of

the Komsomol (Communist Youth Movement), where she worked over half a day. Towards the end of the day Galina met there her former Russian teacher who knew that she was a believer. Galina was suddenly dismissed on the grounds that the previous typist had returned. Galina's sixth attempt to find employment was in a large factory where she was appointed as a secretary. However, when her manager discovered that she was a believer, he sent her to be an apprentice on the assembly line. Galina left the factory and saw a window poster advertising for a typist with a firm called Home Radios. She was given the job. The management soon discovered that she was a believer and decided to dismiss her. Galina's mother went to the public prosecutor's office on the next day to inquire about the propriety of this action. The acting district attorney explained to her that a woman believer cannot work as a typist and recommended she find a different kind of work.

Although the experiences of young believers are not always as bad as this, it is a fact that believers are often confronted by great problems when looking for work. Gifted young believers are exposed to especially difficult inner struggles when choosing work because they are not able to take their aptitudes into account. They are frequently interviewed by the KGB and offered higher education in return for a promise to collaborate with them and keep them informed about the activities of their unregistered church.

The majority of believers in the USSR perform manual jobs, and as conscientious and reliable workers they are valued everywhere, unless some zealous government officer steps in to stir up trouble for them. However, the campaign for the minds of children and young people is extremely intense, and unregistered Baptist families are hit particularly severely by the vindictive laws of recent years.

19
The "Fanatical" Baptists

Regional newspapers in the Soviet Union wage a constant war on believers through feature and news articles. Those articles give us further insight into the official view of Soviet rulers towards believers, particularly those in unregistered churches. They are generally represented as fanatics who want to see and hear nothing except matters connected with their faith and who turn other people into "religious cripples." The following excerpts from recent newspapers have been culled and extracted by the compilers of the *Prisoner Bulletin,* the magazine of the Council of Prisoners' Relatives.

The *Shakhterskaya Pravda* of Prokopievsk, Siberia, reported under the headline "Not for God's Sake, Nor for Men," that Evangelical Baptists, contrary to rumor, were not murderers who crucified people physically. "No!" declared this paper. "No one is attacked with violent force in these churches. These are places where personalities are crucified, living personalities, and preferably young ones."

The article goes on to say that the children of believers become fanatics before they are old enough to go to school and display that fanaticism the moment they arrive at school. "At Regional School No. 16 two girls insolently displayed their 'knowledge' in writing an essay on the origin of life on earth. These girls, named Schaaf and Steinke, ended their essays with the words—'This is not true; God created man!'" The paper added the comment—"If the law punishes such antisocial manifestations as theft and violence, then it should also punish the deeds of those who cripple the personality or spirit of another person. Society loses even more by this kind of violence.''

Believers are frequently depicted as madmen in the newspapers. A Brest newspaper, *Zarya,* gave this description of Baptists: ''They are those who, in the hard years of Hitler's occupation, willingly licked Nazi boots to save their own skins.''

The journalistic campaign against unregistered Baptists is lively, well presented, and, in a way, very well informed. Nearly all the newspaper articles in 1984 distinguished between ''good'' Baptists and ''bad'' Baptists. Quotations from four papers show how this is generally done. The *Slava Krasnodona* printed the following explanatory piece under the heading, ''Not the Way.''

> In 1944 two sects—the Evangelical Christians and the Baptists—united on account of their similarity of faith and rites. The new religious organization was given the name ''Church of the Evangelical Christian Baptists.'' In 1945 a large proportion of the Pentecostal churches amalgamated with them, and in the early 1960s part of the Mennonite sect also joined. The organization has become the largest of all the sects active in our country. It is led by an elected body known as ''The All-Union Council of Evangelical Christian Baptists.'' This controls local churches, publishes a magazine called *The Fraternal Herald,* convenes congresses, and maintains contact with Baptist churches abroad and also with the World Baptist Alliance.

The ''bad'' Baptists emerge as those unreasonable people who for unsavory reasons will not accept this democratically run and world-acknowledged denomination.

The *Vechernyi Kishinev,* the Kishinev evening paper, also published a historical survey of the Baptist movement, drawing attention to the separation of independent Baptists under the heading, ''The Fall of Man!'' The paper stated:

> In the fifties a crisis was becoming clearly visible within the Baptist churches. The irreversible process of the aging of

church members affected Baptists throughout the country. Two-thirds of the followers of the Baptist faith were over sixty years of age. However, a few ardent Baptists felt obliged to explain that phenomenon by external factors rather than by factors within their church. They openly charged that the aging crisis was the direct result of pressure exerted by Soviet law on their churches, and they decided that they must revise their attitude to the laws of the state.

In that way opposition to the All-Union Council of Evangelical Christian Baptists arose from its own ranks. The activities of those opponents went so far that after a while they founded their own self-styled "Council of Evangelical Christian Baptist Churches," in opposition to the All-Union Council. The new council concentrated on setting believers at odds with the "world" and setting the Baptist churches against the state. It aimed to isolate believers from society, produce an anti-social atmosphere in the churches, and provoke believers to commit all manner of infringements of existing legislation.

The evening daily of Chelyabinsk—the *Vechernyi Chelyabinsk*—printed a report in August 1984 headlined "Contrary to Order." It read:

> It is now time to explain who the separatist Baptists (the "Initiatniki") are. They call themselves followers of the Council of Evangelical Christian Baptist Churches. They split off from the main evangelical Christian Baptists in 1961 claiming that the leaders of that organization are too loyal in their conduct towards the worldly authorities. According to the leaders of these religious extremists the churches should not be subject to secular laws.

The Brest newspaper, *Zarya*, returned to the subject with an even more detailed report on the split among the Baptists.

> Early in the 1960s the All Union Council of Evangelical Christian Baptists sent to all its churches an outline of new [Soviet] rules for the churches together with a "letter of instruction for leaders of assemblies." The writers of that circular called upon their fellow believers to bring the activities of their churches fully into line with existing legislation

on religious practices. Immediately a number of individual-
istic extremists and faction leaders showed their true character. In an open letter to their movement they condemned
the All-Union Council for its "loyal conduct towards the authorities" and called for outright violation of Soviet legislation on the holding of religious services.

It is necessary at this point to quote from the All-Union
Council's letter of instruction to church leaders so that readers
can see what the leaders of the separatist group were not prepared to obey. This letter of instruction was originally intended to be a secret document and was addressed only to church
leaders.

> Children of preschool and school age should not normally
> be allowed to attend services of worship. In the past, in-
> fringements of Soviet legislation on worship services oc-
> curred in some of our churches because of insufficient at-
> tention with regard to this matter. There were cases of
> people under eighteen years of age being baptized. Bible
> studies and other gatherings of a special nature were held.
> Poetry recitals were allowed. Outings for believing young
> people took place. Meetings were held for the training of
> preachers. Preachers were allowed to visit from other local
> churches. Funds were raised for various purposes, and
> there were other infringements of Soviet legislation also. All
> that must be removed from our churches and our activities
> must be made to comply with the operative legislation for
> services in our country, to which end we, the pastors of the
> All-Union Council, should be helped by the document "New
> Order for the All-Union Council" and this "Letter of Instruc-
> tion."

Some of the leaders of the registered churches also contribute articles to the Soviet press, claiming that there is no
police activity against Christian believers simply on the
grounds of their being Christians. Pastor Kilmenko, a former
president of the All-Union Council, said in the Kishinev evening paper, "To claim that anyone from the ranks of our

churches or any other churches has been put in the dock simply because he is a believer is nonsense! Soviet legislation does not provide for persecution of citizens merely because of their faith."

In that same article, Kilmenko quotes the Russian orthodox primate of Moscow and all of Russia, who declared:

> There is no kind of public record kept, or statistics kept, of religions in the USSR. There are no questions asked about adherence to a religion when a worker is employed, or in the national census, or in the issuing of personal papers. Believers of all religions, including clergymen, are full citizens of the Soviet state, entitled to take part in the political, economic, and social life of the country.

However, what those religious leaders say is contradicted by other articles written by secular newsmen. In an article entitled "To Improve Atheistic Education," printed in the Moldavian newspaper *Dawn of Communism,* the state campaign against religion is set out very clearly.

> The Plenum of the Central Committee of the Communist Party of the Soviet Union held in June 1983 emphasized with renewed force that the task of defeating the remnants of the religious errors of part of the population remains current. It is known that men are neither born as believers or atheists. Their creed is formed under the influence of various environmental circumstances arising from their manner of life. Reality is assuredly on our side. However, one may not trust that faith in God will die out by itself. Only under the influence of the socialist life-style will it do so. Religion has never yet given up its position in the thoughts and hearts of men voluntarily, and neither will it do so in the future.

In September 1985, the national newspaper *Pravda* published a major article on the need for better atheistic propaganda to counter the menace of religious faith. The article, which was by Dr. R. Platonov, had very special significance as it constituted the first "official" statement on that subject since Mr. Gorbachov's arrival at the helm of the Soviet Union. Would there now be a softening of the antagonism directed at believers? Would there be a less ruthless attitude?

Unfortunately, Dr. Platonov's words gave every indication of a still firmer application of the campaign against belief in God. He stressed that atheist activity must become more forceful than ever, and ordinary members of the public must be stirred up to take their part. Religion, which was to be seen as primitive superstition, must be replaced by a real commitment to Marxist-Leninism, and greatly improved propaganda must be employed to protect the young from religious influences. Atheist agitators must be better trained, and religious communities must be more effectively infiltrated by them.

From *Pravda* it would seem that the policy of recent years is to continue and that the authorities at every level are committed to a program of direct and constant hostility to those who spread the Christian faith. As *Dawn of Communism* reminded its readers—"Religion has never yet given up its position in the thoughts and hearts of men voluntarily."

20

Remember the Prisoners

Leading pastor and member of the Council of Unregistered Baptists, Vasili Ryzhuk, recently recorded an interview in which he was asked the following questions. His replies show the absolute necessity of the pathway that these persecuted believers follow and demonstrate their overwhelming desire to please the Lord Jesus Christ in all that they do.

Was it necessary to be imprisoned for the sake of the gospel? Could you have avoided it, and if so, how?

Suffering for Christ's sake is an expression of my love to Him and of my desire to walk in His footsteps. It is possible to avoid suffering, but to do so you have to break your faithfulness to Jesus Christ. You can no longer proclaim the gospel openly; you have to allow yourself to be forced into the narrow confines of the laws governing religious practices and have to work with the KGB.

Why are believers persecuted, and what fruit does their suffering bring?

Believers are persecuted when they defend the right to openly proclaim the gospel. It is only when persecution fails to intimidate them that they eventually secure the freedom to hold the banner of Jesus Christ high and carry it into the world.

*What effect do the appeals have that are made to the govern-
ment from believers here and abroad? How effective are the
activities of believers in the West, activities such as regular
correspondence with families?*

That activity holds the Soviet government back from even
more cruel measures. I was threatened, for example, that I
would never come out of prison if I did not renounce God.
However, I have been released for the fourth time. The letters
that prisoners and their families receive are seen by them as a
visit from God, as a sign of the unity of the people of God.

Epilogue

*Remember the prisoners, as though in prison with them, and
those who are ill-treated, since you yourselves also are in the
body.*

(Hebrews 13:3, NASB)

The title of this book and the final chapter, *Remember the
Prisoners*, is taken from the letter to the Hebrews, and it spells
out to Christian believers their duty to extend the fullest sympathy and support to all who suffer for the Lord. We are to
think about them, care about them, follow their affairs, pray
for them, and do whatever is possible to relieve them. Will it
one day be said of us, as it was of the readers of the letter to
the Hebrews, "You showed sympathy to the prisoners"?

It must be made clear that the unregistered Baptists are
not the only persecuted group in the USSR. There are many
nonreligious dissidents who display the same enormous courage and who pay very dearly for their views. There are also
ministers and members of other church denominations suffering imprisonment and other forms of persecution. There are
forty prisoners from the ranks of the Russian Orthodox
church, most of whom are imprisoned for human rights activities. There are twenty-six Roman Catholic and twenty Ukrain-
ian Catholic prisoners. Forty-five people from the unregistered
wing of the Pentecostals are in prison, and fifteen from the

Seventh Day Adventist churches. It is therefore recognized that the rigors of persecution extend to many others outside the unregistered Baptist constituency. However, the latter group is currently by far the largest body of churches suffering systematic and determined persecution, having more than 180 pastors and members currently serving sentences.

The unregistered Baptists are certainly unique in having built up a highly effective Bible and Christian literature printing ministry, and they have experienced quite remarkable growth since 1961. For those reasons there is added intensity in the efforts made to imprison leading pastors and workers, and to force churches to register. How badly the authorities must want to find the chairman of the Council of Unregistered Churches—Gennadi Kryuchkov—to confine him under the harshest possible prison regime and permanently break his health and influence.

Believers in the unregistered churches are determined to maintain their witness to the spiritual message of the Bible—the saving power and grace of God to individuals who turn to Him. They feel they have no choice in the matter, for they are called and commissioned by God to be witnesses: "Ye are my witnesses, saith the Lord, that I am God" (Isaiah 43:12). They cannot surrender or mute their commission just because the secular power orders them to do so. They cannot allow people around them to think that the atheistic demands of the secular power carry more weight with them than commands and promises of the omnipotent and glorious God, who they claim to know, love, and obey. Therefore, they obey God and accept the trial of their faith. The authorities expect them to capitulate, but they do not. Neighbors look on and wonder. Will they falter and yield? No, they continue to speak of their Lord, worship and love Him, and they laugh and smile like people who have a source of happiness and help that the atheist knows nothing of.

Such a witness can never be in vain because God has ordained it, and He will cause it to bud and bring forth, in His own time and way, accomplishments far greater than the sufferers could ever ask or think. In England, centuries ago, the fire of martyrdom eventually melted the hearts of the people and broke the tyranny of religious persecution. Already the unregistered Baptists of the USSR have tasted a blessing tantamount to revival in the numbers of souls converted to Christ, particularly among the young, and the number of vigorous churches that have come into being. How much more will God do because His people have loved and obeyed Him to the end?

In the meantime, the Lord says to believers living in freedom—"Remember the prisoners." Let the last word be a recent appeal from the hearts of the wives and mothers of those who are in prison. It is addressed to believers in Christ throughout the world.

> May we not be indifferent to the sufferings of our dear prisoners, those faithful servants of God who have parted with their families and friends, even their lives, for the Lord's honor. Many have been given over to lifelong imprisonment in prisons and concentration camps, damp and forbidding cells. Can we who live in freedom look on without deep feeling, as those sick brethren die behind barbed wire without a glimpse of freedom? Can we be quiet when some of our closest relatives in Christ are given over to virtual execution by imprisonment? Let us pray to God, pleading for their protection and help. Let us also make our appeals to those in power. Let us engage our souls for our dying brethren.

Moody Press, a ministry of the Moody Bible Institute, is designed for education, evangelization, and edification. If we may assist you in knowing more about Christ and the Christian life, please write us without obligation: Moody Press, c/o MLM, Chicago, Illinois 60610.